𝔅𝔢𝔡𝔣𝔬𝔯𝔡𝔰𝔥𝔦𝔯𝔢'𝔰 𝔜𝔢𝔰

War Times & Civil Matters

Brenda Fraser-Newstead

First published November 1996
by
The Book Castle
12 Church Street
Dunstable
Bedfordshire LU5 4RU

© Brenda Fraser-Newstead, 1996.

ISBN 1 871199 23 9

Computer typeset by Keyword, Aldbury, Hertfordshire.
Printed in Great Britain by Bookcraft (Bath) Ltd.

The 'Bedfordshire's Yesteryears' oral history series comprises:
volume 1 :   The Family, Childhood and Schooldays
volume 2 :   The Rural Scene
volume 3 :   Craftsmen and Trades People
volume 4 :   War Times and Civil Matters

Front Cover: Edward Broadbent (centre), one-time Luton
policeman, and First World War veteran, pictured with his four
children c. 1914.
Photo: courtesy Mr J. Crummey

To Jordan, Nathan, Logan
and
Taryn Alice

CONTENTS

FOREWORD
WHAT ARE HOSPICES ?

The modern hospice movement began with the work of Dame Cicely Saunders. She developed new methods in pain and symptom control for patients suffering from cancers, and then went on to found St. Christopher's Hospice in Sydenham, in 1967. Since then, the number of hospices in Britain has increased to well over two hundred, with more being opened every year. They include hospices that provide In-Patient care, Day Care, Out-Patient Care, Home Care, and hospices that are day care centres only. There is even one hospice that has no building at all but provides home care nursing to over a hundred patients at any time.

The name 'Hospice' was first used for places where people were cared for in Christian abbeys and monasteries in medieval times. Then, a hospice was a place for 'the permanently poor, insane, and incurable'. The modern hospice is a place for people who are incurably ill, but 'Hospice' is a word now used to describe a philosophy of care which is patient-centred and holistic. The 'hospice approach' to patients contrasts sharply with the active treatment-focused approach of much of modern medicine, which works hard to cure disease. Care for the patient will also involve care and concern for the family, so that hospice staff say that they do not admit patients, but families. This recognises that people do not live in isolation, but that relationships are at the core of human existence, and that relationships themselves play a large part in the health of individuals.

The need for hospices is closely linked to the growing incidence of cancer as one of the three principal causes of death in Britain. One in fifty people in Britain are living with cancer today, and there is no sign of this number reducing. In addition, hospices care for people suffering from a variety of other terminal diseases, including Motor Neurone Disease and AIDS.

Despite the considerable work and research that has taken place to find both the causes of and cures for cancer, a very high percentage of cancers ultimately prove untreatable. The nature of most cancers is that they often take months and sometimes years to develop fully. The accompanying symptoms are usually painful, embarrassing, and very distressing, both for the patient, and also for the family. Hospice care can control these symptoms and their side-effects, and enable patients to appreciate and enjoy their lives.

Hospices regard dying as a normal process, and they help people to understand and accept what is happening to their loved ones. Hospices are available to all members of the community without regard to religion or other status, and bereavement care forms an active part of the work. This extends the involvement of the hospice within the community well beyond that of direct care for patients.

The great majority of hospices are voluntary charities, with the NHS paying on average only about 34% of their running costs. The majority of hospice running costs each year has to be met from charitable funds. Three hospices in Bedfordshire are all voluntary charities. These are St. John's at Moggerhanger (*A Sue Ryder hospice with twenty beds and a Bereavement Service*), Gladys Ibbett House in Bedford (*A Macmillan Day Centre*), and the Luton and South Bedfordshire Hospice (*ten beds, Day Centre, Home Care and a Bereavement Service*). The amount of charitable funds needed each year to support the Bedfordshire Hospices is in excess of £1,200,000 *or One Hundred Thousand Pounds each month*. For the sake of hundreds of people who need their help every year, please support the hospices.

Martin Johnson, General Manager
Luton & South Bedfordshire Hospice

INTRODUCTION

Researching and writing these four books in the Bedfordshire's Yesteryears series have occupied eight years of my life! These four publications have highlighted and raised funds for four causes in which I have a particular interest:

Research into Alzheimer's disease
Rainbow School in Bromham
The International Fund for Animal Welfare, and
The Hospices at Luton and Moggerhanger

I have enjoyed working on this project and have been fascinated to hear the accounts of times past of which my many contacts have personal knowledge and experience. No doubt I would have continued to write on the subject of social and local history, had I remained in Bedfordshire. Unfortunately personal circumstances have necessitated a move to Bury St. Edmunds. Perhaps someone locally will be inspired to follow in my footsteps and document history as experienced by an older generation of local people.

In time, my efforts to document local history may be seen as an important contribution in this field. It is my hope that for many years to come, my interest in this aspect of history will be shared by many of my readers. If at least my writing enlightens, and gives pleasure, then I shall consider this reward indeed for my efforts.

Brenda Fraser-Newstead

About the Author

Brenda Fraser-Newstead spent many years in the world of commerce and has been a teacher, author and examiner of Business Studies, and a company director. In recent years, however, she has forsaken that involvement and found rewarding work in social welfare and the teaching of children with special needs.

She originates from Wheathampstead in Hertfordshire, but her father was a Lutonian and she herself has lived in Bedfordshire for some twenty-five years.

Acknowledgements

The author wishes to thank, in particular, the contributors to this project, without whose help the book would not have materialised. Thanks also to the very many people, too numerous to mention personally, who have kindly given advice, assistance and support. A special word of thanks to the author's daughter, Yasmina, and to Mr Michael Bates for their continued and valued assistance with editing and proof-reading.

Gratitude also to the following:

Mr E Sabey, Bedford

Mrs H S Brown,
   Moggerhanger

The Wootton Women's
   Institute

Mr J Crummey, Keysoe

Mr A Richer
   (extracts from Bedfordshire
   Police 1840–1990,
   Pub. Hooley)

Mr S Joslin, Feering, Essex

Mrs M Kodulka,
   Pennsylvania, USA

Mr P Hull, Newbury, Berks.

Mr J Marshall, Bedford

Mrs C Richards, Oakley

The Shuttleworth Collection

The Imperial War Museum

Mr & Mrs W Parrott,
   Milton Ernest

Mr C Bourne, Dunstable

Staff at the Goldington
   Social Centre,
   Bedford

Mrs M Glenford, Bedford

Mr J Leech, Dunstable

The Befrienders, Flitwick

WAR TIMES

Barrage balloons in the skies of Britain.
Photo: courtesy The Imperial War Museum.

Evacuee children leaving for a safe home in the country.
Photo: courtesy The Imperial War Museum.

WAR TIMES

Introduction

War times in Bedfordshire, as elsewhere in the country, meant absence of husbands, fathers, brothers, and often the loss of loved ones, or the trauma of life with those returning injured and maimed. For those not able to serve in the Forces, the ARP and Home Guard offered the opportunity of safeguarding the homeland. Production for the war effort, and work on the land, led to greater demand for female labour, and many women found their way into commerce and industry as job opportunities opened up in a way never before

Land Army girls at work, 1942. Photo: courtesy West Sussex County Records Office, Chichester and Garland Collection WSRO c. 1987.

experienced. Many women were recruited to work in the Land Army, to ensure essential food production in times of uncertainty and blockaded imports.

In the first war many families assisted with billeting of soldiers. In the second war evacuees poured into the county to escape heavy bombardment of the towns, cities and centres of industry. Everyone experienced rationing and food shortages, in addition to shortages of other commodities. In an effort to safeguard themselves, many built shelters, of varying types: others made common-sense use of limited resources, sheltering in cellars, under large tables, blacking-out windows, etc. Everyone carried a gas-mask. Prisoners of war arrived: some were allowed to assist civilians with gardening and so on, whilst many helped on the land and at the brickworks.

Searchlights, barrage balloons, aircraft, anti-aircraft fire, bombs, – Bedfordshire saw them all, and although damage was caused and fatalities occurred, Bedfordshire did not suffer to such a degree as did other parts of the country. Nevertheless, when hostilities ceased and celebrations ensued, Bedfordshire's villages and towns were left to mourn their losses.

First World War

'I had been working with my father on various jobs including thatching for a few months when, on August 4th, 1914, Britain declared war on Germany. As a teenager I was very frightened, not so with an old village worthy who, when told that England had declared war on Germany, said "Ah, well, they've got a nice day for it". The war lasted over four years.

Not many days passed before young men from the village left to join His Majesty's Forces. My eldest brother, Fred, who was working as a footman in gentleman's service in Worthing left his employment to join the Forces about the second day of the war. He soon found the difference being in the army!

Only a few weeks elapsed before no less than 30,000

Scottish soldiers, the whole of the 51st Highland Division, came to the town of Bedford for training. At that time horses were the main means of transport for hauling the guns, carriages and wagons. Army officers arrived in the village commandeering all available stabling including most of the kennels of the Oakley Hunt. New sheds began to spring up like mushrooms in suitable fields and these formed part of the hospital for the sick and wounded horses. This was all part of the Veterinary Corps, an off-shoot of the 51st Highland Division.

On route marches which sometimes took place through our village, [Milton Ernest] the line of kilted soldiers marching four deep seemed to be never-ending. Each company was headed with its band of bagpipes and drums. It was a sight I shall never forget and shall certainly never see again.

In 1915 the village seemed to be filling up with men in khaki to look after our horses. Men from farms in neighbouring villages who had any knowledge of horses came to work as civilians and the wages paid were much higher than on the farm, which also was an attraction. After a few weeks or months, an officer would have a talk with the 'civvies; and tell them they would be better off in the army, and, much to their regret later, they would take the King's shilling.

With the main railway line running through the village with its viaducts and bridges, it had to be guarded against enemy saboteurs. In the early days of the war special constables and volunteers did this for a short time; Scout masters who took part wore a red feather in their hat and were part of what was called the Red Feather League. A little later on a squad of soldiers who had seen service abroad and in South Africa came to the village to guard the bridges.

Accommodation had to be found in the village for those men, and I well remember a sergeant coming to see my mother about the billeting of the men and without hesitation he said, "Mrs Parrott, I have heard what a good billet this is and I am putting eight men for you to look after". A discussion took *place, my mother explaining that with just a four-bedroomed cottage and a family, it was impossible to sleep them all, so in the end eight men came for their meals and four of them had to go out to sleep in another cottage. With the four men who slept at our house our bedroom seemed to be full of men and boys. I well remember one night the leg of the soldiers' bed crashing through the floor boards and through the ceiling below into the living room. In the morning we were all amused to see this bed leg sticking through the ceiling. It was after this that our standard of living began to improve due to the additional money which my mother received for looking after, and feeding, the men.*

I ought to mention that soon after the outbreak of the war, King George Vth and Queen Mary evacuated some of their family from Buckingham Palace. As Lady Ampthill was a Lady-in-Waiting to Her Majesty two of the young princes came to the Hall for safety and I well remember them sleeping in a tent near to the river. Two detectives kept watch over them, one by day and the other by night. These detectives were housed in the bothy in the courtyard. All this was kept very secret but at that time I was loaned by my father to the head gardener and so I saw the princes on many occasions.

The Old Bedfords were a company who arrived in the village to guard the railway bridges and viaducts, and, as already mentioned, the men were a mixed bag who had seen service overseas. They came from London, Luton, Bedford, as well as the surrounding districts. One of the eight who were billeted with us went by the name of "Sailor Jack". He went out to sleep at another billet. Jack, in civvie life, had always laid rough and insisted with the landlady that he would rather sleep in her old farm barn than in one of her nice clean beds. She agreed to this and with a heap of clean straw, this was his bed. He was quite happy as he would be returning to this sort of life when the war came to an end. Some years later I went with my father to thatch the roof of a butcher's shop in the village of Sharnbrook. One of the first people we met was

FONDEST LOVE TO DADDY.

Two loving hearts are waiting,
Longing to see you dear,
Feeling so lonely without you,
Wishing that you were near.

Sailor Jack who made his abode in a loft over the stable for a number of years. The approach to the loft was by a step ladder to the doorway from the outside. It was quite dark inside, no windows in the roof and all Jack had was a candle to light him to his bed of bags, sacks and old coats. He later lived in a hutment on the outskirts of the village and a report in the local paper after his death revealed that his name was Jack Bartram and that he had never been in the navy.

The company of old soldiers I have mentioned, were mainly of Scottish origin and had been attached to various Scottish regiments in the past, there being one bugler boy and one drummer boy, neither of which was sixteen years old. They both acted as messengers at headquarters during the daytime and at 10pm the bugler boy would stand almost in the centre of the village to play the Last Post (lights out) with his bugle. This lad had worked in a barber's shop before joining the forces and in his spare time took the opportunity of opening up a barber's shop in the village, hiring one room in someone's house. In the evenings he was almost overcrowded so I acted as lather boy for him and this brought in a little pocket money for us.

After well over four years of war, on 11th November, 1918, armistice was signed much to the relief of everyone. The number of men killed from this small village was twelve and many of those who returned home had been wounded, two of them had each lost a leg.'

WALTER ('REG') PARROTT

'My father was an engineer in the army. At the time he was due to be posted to France he was working on a hospital in Sandwich, Kent. There was an epidemic of influenza (something like Asian flu) and he died from this. Mother said people were dying like flies, and told me how she saw them all lined up in the mortuary with labels round their necks, when she went there to see father. She said what a pitiful sight it was. It was thought the virus had been brought over from the

Continent by returning soldiers. The last time I saw m.
was when he was on leave and came home for two or t
days, before going to France.

After the First World War my mother got a job cleaning a.
office in Bushmead Avenue, Bedford. She also knitted golf
socks for the officers – there were still a lot of army people in
the area – which they wore with the "plus fours". One of my
sisters was a Telegram Girl during the war, working shifts,
and cycling around Bedford delivering telegrams. If someone
was killed in action, relatives would be notified by telegram,
and it was a busy time. She was provided with a navy
uniform piped in red, with a flat round hat and a leather belt
containing a pouch for the telegrams, which were collected
from the Bedford Post Office in Dame Alice Street, opposite
the almshouses, and delivered around Bedford. My uncle,
Mr Charles Thompson (my mother's brother), was Head
Postmaster in Bedford.

During the war there were a lot of Scotsmen in this area. In
fact, the war started on 4 August 1914 and a few weeks later
thirty thousand Scottish soldiers (the entire 51st Highland
Division) arrived in Bedford for training. My eldest sister fell
in love with one of the sergeants called Sandy. They
corresponded for some time, but he was later killed in France.
These soldiers bought everything they could lay their hands
on in the general shop in Bower Street, which was opposite
our home. My mother had a sergeant and another officer
billetted with us.

I had never seen so much meat and food as there was
available to us at this time. Every morning a cart full of meat
came round and this was all provided free of charge in
addition to pay for billeting the soldiers. From this meat
mother saved dripping, which I had to take up the road in a
big bowl to a neighbour who had nine kiddies to feed. I went
to school with one of the girls. The mother said this dripping
kept them going during the war years. There was another cart
loaded with Sunlight soap, piled up like bricks, and long tins

Irene Cornwell's parents at 108 Bower Street, Bedford. In the background is the soldier they billeted, talking to little Irene.

of corned beef.

At the top of Bower Street was a piece of green, and the Scottish soldiers had dances here. I remember that it was wonderful, bagpipes and swaying kilts. So romantic. It was a magnificent sight to see them parading on Sundays. There were many soldiers from different places – they didn't all wear kilts.

During this period of billeting, I had three sisters at home and two brothers. All the children had to help out at home but we got on well with our two soldiers. Further up the road there were a rough lot and one or two girls got pregnant by some of them. I don't know what became of these girls and their babies, but there was a Mother and Baby Home in Hurst Grove, Bedford, a church home for unmarried mothers. I myself worked there in the 1960s for six years. Many girls were not allowed to take their babies home and a lot of children were adopted from this place. There were many tears at times.'

EDITH IRENE CORNWELL

'During the First World War my mother had two or three lots of soldiers billeted with her, and I remember that one of them got burnt when they were doing exercises in the fields up Honeyhill. We even had a family living with us at one time, Welsh people, with lots of little children.'

WINIFRED BURTON

'I was born on 3 March 1900 at 31 Ashton Street, Luton, where I lived until I was married. On the wall of the house was a Roll of Honour plaque, displaying the names of all the men who had served in the Great War, highlighting those who had been wounded or killed. There was a small metal vase attached at the side and mother kept this filled with fresh flowers until she moved away through ill health in 1949. The street name was later changed to Gillam.

I began work in an iron moulding foundry. The war broke

out shortly afterwards and my foreman had a son going to the Modern School and he pestered his father to let him leave to join up. He got killed within six weeks, and there were several cases in the shop like that, and I felt very guilty and left. They told me not to leave because I'd got a war badge to say I was in war work, but I felt this wasn't enough. When I went to join up I was not passed because of my eyes, so then I was out of work and took a job in the hat factory.

I am a member of the Harpenden Western Front organisation, and am interested in the First World War. The organiser is an authority on the first war and we watch old films and if anyone has been in the action they stand up and talk about it. Someone brought along a German uniform from this war for us all to see. It's very nostalgic. My daughter is also quite an authority on this war.'

FRANK CHAPMAN

'My father was a soldier in the Royal Fusiliers during the First World War. This was the only regiment to have walked through the city of London with fixed bayonets. He returned from the First World War where he saw action in Russia and France, and where he was wounded and lost the sight of one eye. After demobilisation he went back to general farm work.

When I was about fifteen my father developed TB which we always believed was caused through gassing in the war, – the use of mustard gas that is. This had affected his breathing. With my father's meagre pension from the forces, my parents saved enough money to buy the home in Renhold Road, Top End, Renhold, where I am still living.'

WILLIAM CONSTANT

'During wartime, there were ten soldiers compulsorily billeted at my parents' home in Radwell. They had to guard the viaduct over the river at Radwell, to prevent sabotage, as this carried the main railway line. These soldiers nursed me and played with me, so my mother said, dressed me up in their helmets. *Some of the men slept in the house, some in the barn adjoining the house. Each day mother cooked twenty-one dinners for hers and other soldiers and sent these down to the railway! My mother recalled to me in later years that these men would do anything for a pint of beer.'* IVY FLUTE

'My husband was on the searchlights in the First World War, and I met him for the first time at Edgware, during the Peace Celebrations. This was on bonfire night. We courted for about six years.' SARAH HILLS

'During the war Biscot Camp was largely the stopping off place for troops going to France. People noticed the difference in the troops. Big burley men were everywhere in 1914 but by 1918 the men were physically much less fit. These were observations made by people who watched men marching up and down Biscot Road. There was a mill there at one time, – Biscot Mill – and the camp. During my time it has been joined on to Luton via Biscot Road, but was probably a village previously.' CLAUDE HORWOOD

'During the First World War I was sent to Coventry to work in the arsenal making shells. At this factory they made the big guns for the ships. I worked on a capstan, and had to stand on a box to reach it. This was men's work until they were conscripted into the army. The Zeppelins used to come over and all the factories – which had glass roofs – were plunged into darkness. This seemed to me to be the only threat, I didn't consider any other danger working in munitions. I never felt threatened, apart from the Zeppelins. I went back to Coventry after the Second World War and it had been completely flattened.' MARY JEFFS

Wartime poster encouraging people to eat less bread. Photo: courtesy The Imperial War Museum.

'I was the youngest of eight children and my parents owned the bakery called 'Britannia Bakery' which was on the corner of High Street South and Britain Street in Dunstable, but which everyone knew as "England's Bakehouse". This is now occupied by a firm of accountants. I was a young girl when the First World War started and we had about thirty of forty soldiers billeted with us during the war. We were visited by the Billeting Officer, who came to count the number of rooms which we had. He chalked "C3" on the outside of the house, and this meant that we had to have three soldiers. They only slept with us as they had their own mess at the White Swan Yard.

Everything was in short supply during the war and my father was not allowed to sell bread which was under twelve hours old. This was because there was less demand for old bread!'

ELSIE ENGLAND

'In June 1916 I remember meeting a school friend of mine delivering evening papers. She said "Lord Kitchener has been drowned: it's in the paper". I hurried home to tell my father what I had heard. He wouldn't believe it but gave me a penny to purchase a paper. There was the report. Kitchener of Khartoum had gone down in the cruiser "Hampshire", torpedoed in the Orkneys on her way to Russia. Bear in mind there were no telephones, radios or television in those days to convey news, good or bad, to country districts.

I still think of those men of the village who served in the First World War. One was Neville Taylor, now ninety years of age. He served in France. Up to a very short time ago he could be seen cycling to Maulden Post Office to fetch his pension. He was our postman for many years and he also mended shoes for the people in the village.

Another veteran of the First World War is Albert Sadler, now eighty-seven years of age. Up to a very few weeks ago I observed him cycling up to his allotment before 8 o'clock in the morning. He was in an army camp at Hastings during the First World War – in 1918. My husband was also in the same camp but they did not know one another then and I of course did not know either of them. Albert Sadler was sent to Ireland and my husband went with the Army of Occupation to Germany. We met when my husband and I came to Maulden in 1929. Mr and Mrs Sadler have always been good friends and neighbours.'

GLADYS WALLIS

'During the First World War there were soldiers billeted at the big house (Lord and Lady Thynne's residence) [Haynes]. Mules were used for transportation and you could see them grazing in the grounds of the house. I used to pass by with my school friends when we walked to Church End School, and we often saw the soldiers driving them, and drawing the waggons.'

BEATRICE WEBB

'During the First World War there was a camp near Colmworth and many Scottish soldiers were billeted there. I can still see them marching around, in my mind's eye.

There was a spate of illness which occurred just after the First World War and assumed epidemic proportions, being particularly prevalent in London, and killing many people. I was taken ill with the fever when I was eighteen and was very poorly for five years. Many of my friends in the villages died with the same illness.

During the wars and period of rationing, there was no food shortage on the farm. When my father gave up farming At Rectory Farm, my brother and I took on Abbey Farm, Elstow. This was along Ampthill Road. I ran the home and he farmed. During the war-time there were evacuees to help with the farm work, and a load could be brought out by request, to assist.'

EVELINE STANTON

'My father was in the 11th and 13th Hussars, and he married my mother in 1910, obtaining consent to marry only after his fiancée had produced three references stating that she was of reputable character. He had left the regiment and was working as a baker when they married, but was still a Reserve. He was proud of his association with the regiment and loved Ireland, where they were based.'

FREDA BROWN

'On 4 August 1914 the First World War was declared, at the start of the harvest. There was a lot of talk about the war but I didn't really understand what was going on, but then my eldest brother joined up in September and I came to realise what it was all about. My brother had been working on another farm, enlisted and was instructed to be back at Kempston Barracks at a certain time, where the recruits were issued with one blanket each and had to sleep in the barrack yard. He was sent to France and was wounded in the foot just before the armistice was signed.

We were rationed during the war and I remember the bread being terrible, as bakers had to use second-rate flour. We had honey sugar instead of jam, which we ate on bread. I believe we were better off during the Second World War than during the First World War, in this respect.'

HORACE WELCH

'I remember one time on the farm during the war. British Drug Houses collected in-foal mares' water, and Alec Sawford, the Horseman, always had

Horace Welch's eldest brother, Edwin, shortly after joining up in the First War, looking splendid in his red tunic and blue trousers.

a bucket on his plough, for collecting it. One evening he took the lid off and struck a match to see how much he had in the bucket and it ignited and flared up to the stable roof and burnt his face real badly. I suppose it was the ammonia in it.'

WINIFRED ALLAN

'My father was of Scottish descent and born in Norfolk. My mother originally came from Northampton. My father was in the 1st Bedfordshire Regiment 5th Division (L/C Brown, Signaller). He then went onto the Reserve and was working as *a postman in Aylesbury, where I was born just before the First World War.*

George Brown
with his mother
and baby brother.

At the outbreak of the war my father, being a Reserve, was called up for active service into the Beds and Herts Regiment, and I still have a photograph of the Regiment in Colchester, taken at about this time, when the first British expedition was preparing to go to France. I also have a letter which my father wrote to me whilst in the trenches. This contains a very moving message of love and concern, written at a time of despair and desperation. He survived this terrible ordeal and

My Darling Boy George

I now take the pleasure in writing to you and wishing you a happy birthday.

My Dear Son. When you are older and able to read you will be able to realise where your Daddy was when he wrote this letter to you. Well my Dear Boy I am out in France fighting for you and your Dear Mother and our homes and King and Country and when you are going to school you will learn how we fought the Germans. My Dear Boy if anything happens to your Daddy in this war I ask you to look after your Dear Mother and to love her always and to keep her from all harm as your Daddy has always looked after you and Mother and loved you both with a warm heart whilst he was with you. Dear Son I hope you will always be a good boy and grow up to be a man and also to pray and to thank God for his goodness to us as your Daddy trusts in him and thanks the Lord that he will return Daddy safely home to you both.

Now I think you will be able to read this some day and with my fondest love and kisses

I remain   Your Ever Loving Daddy

George's father's letter to him on his first birthday, written whilst in the trenches.

after repatriation, we all moved to 50 Foster Hill Road in Bedford, and we have lived in Bedford ever since.

The village postman – George's father.

My father suffered injuries, being wounded four times during the war and had shrapnel in his knee for about twenty years. He was awarded several medals, also the Mon's Star Bar and Rose. He suffered severe depression after his return to civilian life, drank heavily every night and refused to talk about his war-time experiences. He then became a Christian and was baptised in 1928, and from that time onwards he was a changed man. He resumed work for the Bedford Post Office, where he worked altogether for thirty-three years.'

GEORGE BROWN

Three brave young men, all of whom perished in action in the First World War.
Photo: courtesy Mrs Marjorie Glenford.

Menu for Xmas Dinner

ROAST PORK.   ROAST BEEF.
APPLE SAUCE.   SUET PUDDING.
SAGE & ONION STUFFING.

POTATOES.   CABBAGE.   PARSNIPS.

XMAS PUDDING.
RUM SAUCE AND CUSTARD.

ORANGES.   APPLES.   FIGS.   NUTS.

BISCUITS.   CHEESE.   CELERY.

BOTTLED BEER.   BOTTLED STOUT.   DRAUGHT BEER.

VIN BLANC.   CITRON.   LEMON SQUASH.

CIGARS.   CIGARETTES.

Concert Programme

CHAIRMAN. Captain BEATTY, R. A. S. C.

ARTISTES

Gnr. CLARKE.	Sentimental Song.
Pte. COLLINS.	Banjo Selections.
Cpl. JACKSON	Song. Selected.
Pte. ALEFOUNDER	Comic Song.
Pte. WESTON.	Monologue.
Pte. (Tatcho) PADGETT . . . . /	
Pte. (Taffy) POWELL . . . . \	Duet.
Pte. SELBY.	Descriptive Song.
Pte. EMERY	Sentimental Song.
Cpl. LEWIS	Serio Comic Song.
L/Cpl. MAY	Song. Selected.
Pte. GARNETT	Dance.
Pte. CAMP	Serio Comic Song.
Pte. IRISH	Song. Selected.
Cpt. HAYS	Comic Song.
Pte. WORGER	Song.

Under the direction of :   Pianiste :

Cpl. LEWIS and Pte. CAMP.   **L/Cpl. MASON.**

Frederick Drake served in the forces in France during the First World War with the 15th Auxiliary Bus Company.
The company had not been demobilised by Christmas 1918, and

his granddaughter still has the menu and programme of events organised in celebration of that special Christmas.
Courtesy: Mrs P Headey.

The Depression

The depression which existed during the inter-war period, saw conflict in industrial relations nationwide. There were strikes among engineers, railwaymen, cotton workers, Yorkshire miners, foundry workers and in many other industries. The trade-union movement was growing and the unions were becoming more powerful. One dispute which occurred in the engineering industry in 1922 involved forty-eight unions and arose over the refusal of the unions to permit unlimited overtime at the employers' discretion. The three-month dispute ended with the unions forced to return to work after the exhaustion of their funds, and indeed, lack of funds forced many other unionists back to work. In the coal industry, conflict over demands for nationalisation and employers' attempts to enforce wage cuts, led to the dispute which escalated into the General Strike of May 1926. An outraged miners' leader challenged the employers with 'Not a minute on the day, not a penny off the pay'. However, the strike created conditions of severe poverty for many miners' families, and there was a real fear of starvation. The government, with Winston Churchill Chancellor of the Exchequer, stood firm and The General Strike resulted in victory for the government, and subsequently, the 1929 election brought Labour to power.

Obviously some sectors of the community fared worse than others, but the general trend during this period, – when never less than one-tenth of the working population were unemployed – was towards poverty and hardship.

'This was a time which it is not easy to forget. Thousands of people were thrown out of work. Some who were lucky could draw unemployment benefit, but many people couldn't, including myself. This depression took place after the General Strike in 1926 when miners and railwaymen came out, I suppose, for more money. One feature of the difficult years in the 1920s was the hunger march of men from Jarrow to

London, to draw attention to the plight of men willing and eager to work but for whom there was no employment available. The march was headed by Miss Ellen Wilkinson, MP.

People seemed to stop spending on their roofs [thatch] and we were coming to a complete standstill. My brother left me to work on a market gardener's farm, and I took on any job that was forthcoming such as hedge trimming, pea picking, muck spreading – anything to keep me occupied.

Farm subsidies came to an end for corn growing, and agriculture soon began to feel the pinch. Prices for what the farmers were producing fell rapidly, and therefore men's wages were reduced accordingly. During the depression, agriculture went to the dogs and a good farmer – after working hard all the year – had a job to make both ends and the middle meet. In fact, I knew of one farmer who admitted to losing £100 a year for six years, this being a large amount of money in those days. Many farmers left their farms and in some cases sold them cheaply. The unoccupied farms soon went derelict and most of the fields grew nothing but rubbish and bushes, making good harbour for rabbits and foxes. It was around this time that unemployment was much worse and in order to keep myself at work I undertook to repair the thatched roofs of some farm buildings. I worked for eleven weeks and my bill came to about £13. The farm labourers' pay at that time was £1.10s.6d (£1.52) per week. After this, work seemed to pick up again and this trend lasted until 1939, when Britain again declared war on Germany.'

WALTER (REG) PARROTT

'I still remember the Jarrow hunger march. In the 1920s men marched from Jarrow to London to draw attention to the plight of the unemployed. The marchers slept the night at Goldington Road School on their way to London. No end of them came, and they were issued either with new boots or new blankets before they continued. The march was headed by

Miss Ellen Wilkinson MP. Then came the General Strike in 1926, when the miners and the railwaymen came out.'

EDITH CORNWELL

The Jarrow marchers in Bedfordshire. Photos by kind permission of the Hulton-Deutsch Collection (from Times Gone By, Ed. John Gaisford, pub. Marshall Cavendish Books Ltd.).

'I started at Beech Hill [School, Luton] when I was five, and left at fourteen. I didn't enjoy school and wanted to leave. There weren't any leaving examinations. There was a slump at the time, and I worked at the Diamond, fitting gas cookers at 4d each. My brother lived and worked in Leagrave and he encouraged me to get a trade behind me. Many boys went into blind alley jobs and were sacked at 16–18. If you were unemployed there was dole money but it was means tested. The Labour Party was beginning then: it was Tories and Liberals. Everyone disliked the Tories for not helping the poor.

When I was fifteen or sixteen I started work at the foundry, the Alliance, making machinery and machine parts. It was work for Vauxhall, Commer, SKF Co and Kents, for local industries. You could get into the foundry easily and there were no apprenticeships. Apprenticeships had to be paid for in those day, and my grandmother couldn't afford it. Foundry work was unpopular with young boys. I moved to Brown and Greens and then to Hudsons. I was tied to the foundry because of the slump. If you were unemployed you had to sign on the labour every day. You could be suspended for six weeks if you left work without good reason. This happened to me after a dispute with a foreman, and for answering back. I went before a tribunal but it didn't help, it wasn't fair.

It was very hard work in the foundry, real hard work: 18/- a week, if you were sick (this was before the National Health), and 18/- a week on the dole. I earned 11/- a week

Tom, taking a break.

when I first started work there. I cycled to work, and it was a forty-six-and-a-half hour week, with no pay for holidays. You had to save up for that and only one week was allowed, and Bank Holidays.'

THOMAS WILLIAM WOODCOCK

Second World War

'In addition to myself, seven of my brothers and sisters saw active service of one sort or another in uniform during the war, the exception being my elder sister Mary, who was married to a Naval Officer and had two small children at the time.

Having joined the RAF in 1941 I was subsequently commissioned as a pilot. In 1943 whilst flying a Lancaster over Germany, I was attacked and was fortunate to survive a forced landing. Having eluded capture for a period of several months, I was eventually arrested by the Gestapo, and was only liberated at the time of the Russian advance. I was later involved, as a commissioned officer serving with the Coastal Command, in the Berlin Airlift, flying with a squadron of Sunderland flying boats and ferrying in supplies.I was later promoted to the rank of Wing-Commander.

After leaving Preparatory School I was sent to Uppingham in Rutland, and was a pupil there in 1940 at the time two of my brothers were killed in action. My family have since installed a magnificent commemorative stained glass window in Felmersham church, in honour of these, and a third brother who sadly died in 1942.

The interior of Felmersham's seven hundred year old church was aglow from the rays of the setting summer sun when the Bishop of St. Albans, the Rt. Rev. F. M. Gresford Jones, unveiled and dedicated a stained-glass window in the east wall on Wednesday evening.

The window commemorates three sons of Sir Richard Wells, Bart, and Lady Wells, of Felmersham

*Commemorative window installed in Felmersham Church by
Sir Richard and Lady Wells in memory of three of their sons
and of their nurse, Miss Cooper.*

Grange, all of whom were lost in action during the 1939–45 war, and the lady who was their nurse – Miss B. M. Chapman.

Set above the altar, the window depicts a central figure of Christ with the Virgin Mary and St. Christopher on His right, and St. Thomas and St. James on His left.

The names of the Virgin and the Saints correspond with those the window commemorates; Miss Beatrice Mary Chapman, Lieut. Com. Christopher Hayward Wells, R.N., Sqd. Ldr. James Michael Wells, and Major Thomas Capper Wells.

Miss Chapman was nurse at Felmersham Grange for more than thirty years; she died in June 1944. Sqd. Ldr. Wells and Lieut. Com. Wells were lost within a month of each other. In May 1940 Sqd. Ldr. Wells was reported missing from a bombing raid over Holland, and Lieut. Com. Wells was reported killed in action in the following month. He was lost in the aircraft-carrier Glorious, which went down in northern waters. Major Wells, who was a member of the Beds and Herts Regiment was lost at Singapore in 1942.

The theme of the service, conducted by the Vicar (the Rev. A. L. Martin), was of praise and rejoicing. "We rejoice as we think of those who have passed on", said the Bishop in his address. "Rejoicing is exactly the right word, for they have passed on in service, giving their all".

The new window replaces one in memory of Thomas Abbot Green (1855) which was damaged during the 1939–45 war.

(Bedfordshire Times & Standard, 8 June 1951)

St. Christopher, St. Thomas and St. James are shown as patron and name Saints of my three brothers, and the figure of St. Mary is shown as the patron and name Saint of our old *family nurse. As my brothers belonged to one of the three Services, the patron Saint of each Service is shown as a demi-figure beneath each of the men Saints – thus below St. Christopher, as Christopher was a sailor, is St. Nicholas, Patron of Sailors; below St. Thomas, St. George, Patron of Soldiers; and below St. James, St. Michael, Patron of Airmen.*

I left the Forces in 1956, shortly before the death of my father, which came rather suddenly, after a stroke.'

OLIVER WELLS

'The events of the Second World War are still quite fresh in my mind: Chamberlain's visit to Munich, the formation of the ARP, the declaration of war, and the resignation of Chamberlain to make way for Churchill, Dunkirk, and Churchill's famous speech ("We shall fight them on the beaches . . .") are unforgettable. In the village several buildings, including Harrold Hall, were taken over by the Second Survey Regiment. I made many friends among these soldiers, and they were the answer to many female prayers! I vividly recall the air raid on Coventry, for most of the German bombers seemed to fly over Harrold. The only bomb to drop on the village left a large crater at Buildings Farm. London, however, was a different story. I remember going up to Bermondsey on New Year's Day 1944 to find London Transport at a standstill and many fires still burning. With the entry of the United States into the war, the noise of Flying Fortresses taking off fully loaded became a familiar sound. My wife and I had many friends among the crews and we spent many an anxious time awaiting their safe return.

During the war some things were in short supply, and when it ended, it was good to be able to obtain bananas, oranges, grapefruit and such things again, and to buy as much meat as we wanted. We wouldn't have starved in the village, we could get essential foodstuffs, and in fact we got so tired of rabbits we used to bury them in the garden rather than cook them.'

ARTHUR 'LOL' THEW

'After I left school I did a short spell of farm work, then went to the Britannia Works in Bedford and later to Cardington to work in the workshop with the blacksmith, and got to do nearly as well as he did. Then I joined the army and this was where I really got down to blacksmithing. I was sent on a course at London Polytechnic.

In the army you had to make horseshoes, and fit a shoe. The army has certain places where there are still horses. I was posted to Egypt with the Third Infantry Brigade. If a spring broke on a vehicle you had to make a new one. This is all smithing.

Private Bill Constant.

There were about twenty horses where I was posted, a lovely spot like an oasis, called Sarafan, in Palestine. I had to keep these horses shod. I was there for about a year.

I came through the trouble in Egypt, through North Africa, to Salerno. From Salerno in Italy I went up to Naples. You could smell death but there was no word that it was imminent, that a battle would rage. This is where I got tanked. I got one straight in the ribs and the gash wouldn't heal up so it was cauterized and I had to soldier on. We were getting pretty short of troops by then. There was a day of reckoning for us: it wasn't all one-sided.

Our convoy had to pull into Malta into a harbour, a natural harbour. We had to draw in there because of the

U-boats. We were not there many days, not long before we boarded one of the 10,000 tonners, boats that the Americans built. They were all welded together, not rivetted. I think they were all named after a president. We slept in hammocks and all at once we were awakened, we were steaming towards Sicily. We got into battle gear. The end of the ship lets down, you get out on the ducks, as far as you can, and then you scramble in the water. This was just after Mount Etna erupted by the way. We landed on Sicily. There was not much opposition. We stayed a matter of a few days and then went on the boats again and were pushed off the Straits of Messina and up towards Salerno where we landed. All hell broke out. HM War Sprite gave a broadside to cover our landing. Near Cassino there is a large cemetery, – quite a few went under there. Some Bedfordshire men lost their lives including Jack Swan, who was a local man and an old school pal of mine. This was where I got my lot, near Cassino. It was really the turning point of the war. They tried to get through to Anzio, further up the coast. It was as though death was in the air, a weird kind of silence and then you couldn't hear yourself for the heavy guns. I was taken to a place near Naples, a post for rehabilitation. We had to pass through Cassino on the way and it was like a place of death. Great big trees were split in two and there were rats like cats and the place stank, absolutely, stank of death and rotting.

On September 18, (1943) after 9 days of fighting, the Germans pulled back from the beachhead. Although they had yielded the Allies a lodgment, they had not been defeated. Indeed, their withdrawal was part of an established plan to fall back to positions in the northern Appennines . . .

The British, in the heavy fighting around Salerno, the Montecorvino airport and Baltipaglia, had suffered even heavier casualties, a total of 5,500 killed, wounded and missing in action. But the successful conclusion of the first large-scale opposed landing on the European continent, the Salerno operation, which had almost collapsed when the Germans came within two miles of pushing the Allied Army back into the sea, now meant that they were in Italy – and Europe – to stay, and control of the Mediterranean was in their hands.

From WORLD WAR II: THE ITALIAN CAMPAIGN,
by Robert Wallace and the Editors of Time Life Books
© 1978 Time-Life Books Inc.

I was then posted back to Palestine.

In 1947, after being discharged from the army, I went into the Civil Service with the Air Ministry, later called the MoD, at Cardington, and was there until I retired. The airframe for the R100 was still there when I started.'

WILLIAM CONSTANT

'I did have one or two interesting missions as a commercial pilot. The first was to take the diplomatic bag to Prague on September 26, 1938. It was an interesting trip because Prague had been blackened out, and the troops had been mobilised. the Minister was Mr Newton and the Consul Mr Pettit. Having delivered the bag to Mr Newton, as I had been up since 3am and was very tired, he invited me and my radio operator, Jimmy Elmslie, to sleep in his sitting room in the afternoon. In the evening I accompanied Mr Pettit around various buildings in Prague seeking out any British people who wished to return to England, as we were scheduled to leave in the early hours of the following morning. We ended up with a complete complement of ten people and returned without any trouble the next day.

The other adventure which was of interest was two days later when I took the Daily Express reporting staff including Vernon Bartlett, to Munich in time to see some of the celebrities arrive at the airport in preparation for the meeting with Hitler. A friend of mine called Preston was flying Lord Londonderry who at the time was the Minister for Air.

Preston and I got together and went round the centre of Munich having a look to see what was going on. I returned to the hotel where Preston was staying and we were sitting down late in the evening having a cup of coffee when Lord Londonderry joined us. He had been to the conference with Hitler and I said "How have things been going today" and he looked at me and replied, "It could not have been worse; there is certain to be a war", which proved to be only too correct.

I have flown a variety of commercial and World War I and II aircraft including Blenheims, Mark I and IV, Lysander, Hudsons, Ansons, Armstrong Siddeleys, the Bolton & Pail Defiant, and the Blackburn Botha – an aircraft which had several built-in death traps, one being that the petrol supply could easily be turned off as the pilot squeezed in with his chute on.

I did a lot of flying for the searchlights during the war, – that is providing practice for the personnel operating the search-lights – very boring.

My friend and companion, Richard Shuttleworth, lost his life in August 1940 at the age of thirty-one. He had been sent on a fighter course at RAF Benson near Oxford

Searchlights in operation, 1943.
Photo: courtesy The Imperial War Museum.

and had been on circuits and bumps (touch-downs) at night. I do not know the exact deails but believe that Richard had been instructed to do a certain number of circuits and landings and having told the Control Tower he was signing off, was required to do another circuit and landing as he had not completed the time. On take-off the engine stalled and he collided with a hill at the side of the runway.

At the outbreak of the Second World War – 1940 in fact – Richard was on a fighter course at Turnhill and I was at the Air Observer School at Cheltenham, and I flew up to see him. He was in good form and had taken a mobile workshop there and was still working on cars. Although he had done quite a lot of flying as an amateur pilot, I don't think that he had had enough experience of flying on instruments, but I may be wrong. I believe the RAF were certainly to blame, to some degree. It was a terrible waste of life. His mother started the Shuttleworth College in his memory.'

JIMMY EDMUNDS

'I was working at the Igranic in Bedford from 1939–1942 and then everyone of twenty or over was called up for conscription. I had an army medical and the day I was to have been taken to Devises, I had a telegram telling me to return to my employment. The mayor of Bedford worked at Allens, and he was also told to return to his employment because these companies were on priority work for the war effort.

In 1942 they brought out an order making it possible for men to do more for the war effort. I applied, and was sent to Portsmouth, wiring and testing mines. I had an eight-week course at Lee Park, Havant, where they designed the mines. About eighteen months later I was transferred to the British Tabulating Company in Letchworth which the Admiralty had taken over. The British Tabulating Company were building scramble decoding machines. It was all top secret work. I stayed on that work until the end of the war and returned back to my old firm in 1946.'

PERCIVAL 'GEOFF' SHERWOOD

'My lad was in the Second World War. He sent ten-page letters home and always let me know where he was. He was very clever. He would always put in a clue as to where he was, like mentioning the Bayeaux tapestries. One of my brothers was just the same. He stayed at a rest camp named Albert, in France, and instead of signing his name Samuel he signed it "Albert".'

FRANK CHAPMAN

'During the Second World War a bomb fell on some allotments and caused a blast in Honeyhill Road, where we were living at that time, and our home suffered considerable damage. I assume the intended target was either the gas installation or the barracks.'

WINIFRED BURTON

'I was born in 1937 and my sister in 1939, and I can still remember the domed-shaped egg-pod that she had to be laid in. They were issued for all babies as they were obviously too small to wear gas masks. Gas masks had to be carried back

Wootton school children with gas masks c. 1940.

and forward to school all the time. Drilling at school included evacuation of the school and assembly in the underground shelter in the playground. There was a certain point on the way to school – Fountains Road to Denbigh Road – and if you reached that (Biscot Mill) you had to run home if the sirens went. If you had passed that point when you heard the siren sound, you had to continue to school, which was Denbigh Road School. Our mothers must have been worried to death.

The first day I went to school my father, who was a butcher in Fountains Road, took me seated in a basket on the front of his carrier bike, his delivery bike! I was five then. My father had a purpose-built shop with white tiles from floor to ceiling. He started there in 1939 after moving from Stevenage. He had been in business with his father previously. The war was his saving grace, because all the customers had to register with a butcher and the ration books had to be marked when they had had their ration. He didn't have to tout for business, it came to him. The day he opened, by the time he met the payment on the scales and the cold room, he reckoned he had £1.10/- left between him and mother! Most of our neighbours served in the forces and father was the only man left. If the wives needed help with a burst pipe or anything, they came running to dad for help. The shop didn't open Mondays. His meat came from Luton on a Tuesday, his allowance for the number of customers he had. So Monday was his killing day. All the people who were fattening chickens and rabbits and hadn't the courage to kill, brought them up for him to deal with. The rest of Monday he spent baking in the shop. Offal was not on ration and it could be delivered with the meat. It was often condemned in fact and didn't arrive. So his customers had a fair share, he turned it into faggots and Tuesday morning there would be a queue outside, of women standing with bowls ready, to get faggots off-ration. He also baked Cornish pasties, again off-ration. Then someone would go in Saturday saying their son was coming on leave and he would give them our meat and we ended up at the Royal Hotel for lunch on

Sunday. You could get a meal, but what was described as chicken looked and tasted much more like rabbit! The Royal Hotel was on the corner of Midland Road and Old Bedford Road: the building is still there but it's not a hotel now.

When we went to school we had our satchel on one arm, gas mask on the other, and a handkerchief soaked in cologne or Evening in Paris. Each lamp-post had got a metal pig bin chained to it and the lid was chained separately. People had to put anything suitable for pigs to eat in these bins – vegetable peelings and so on, and by the time we came out of the school the lid wouldn't fit and there were wasps and flies all over it. It stank. On the opposite side was an incinerator which contained rags which were doused with paraffin and lit at night to make a smoke screen over Luton so the enemy bombers couldn't locate it. It caused an awful stink and we had to hold our handkerchief over our mouth as we passed by.

We all had black-out: there was no light at night. We children were pushed in to the cupboard under the stairs when the sirens went. It was the broom cupboard, which still contained brooms and polishes. There was a mattress there for us to sit on. Such an awful smell of brasso and wax polish. My parents stood at the back door and watched the bombers go over, mainly to bomb Coventry.

We spent a lot of time in the underground shelters at Denbigh Road School, and they were breeze-block lined, with wooden benches. We were packed in tightly so the boys kicked your ankles, pulled your hair. Your hair would catch on the breeze block and you felt itchy, and the place smelled damp. We spent hours singing songs led by the teachers. All the teachers were coming up to retirement, I don't remember any young staff at all. When I got older there was an overspill and they took over the chapel at St. Margaret's and we had classes in there. Miss Boyd came from Flitwick. She had a car and one day they bombed Commer Cars in Leagrave Road. There was no warning that day and we were told to get under our desks. Someone fetched Miss Boyd to carry the wounded to

Luton and Dunstable Hospital. Two hours later we were still under our desks, no-one had told us to go home! That was discipline! In fact we were all shocked. The bombs made such a horrendous noise, as they fell in the next road.

Vauxhall was bombed and as the factory workers ran out the planes came down and machine-gunned them. We had friends working there in one of the factories. There was a lot injured. They were making Churchill tanks at Vauxhall and it was obviously the place to bomb, a good target. In Leagrave Road there was SKF Co which manufactured things for the war, and Commer Cars. We were quite vulnerable there. There was a dairy shop at Bishopscote and we often paid a ha'penny for an Oxo cube to eat on the way home, as there was sweet rationing. Sweets were rationed by money, not weight. You could buy 6d-worth, a week or something like that, and when your book was marked you got nothing until the following week. Clothes were on ration and it went on after the war. At the age of eleven I had to have boys shoes and ex-WRAF shirts with stiff collars, but they were far superior to school shirts.

I remember the trips to the grocers with mother, another corner shop in St. Augustine's Avenue where we were registered, run by the two Miss Whites. My brother was born in 1945 and we wheeled him around in his pram. Our bread ration was half an uncut loaf, and we carried the shopping home on the pram. My brother used to put his fist in the open end and had eaten half of it by the time we got home! Butter ration was 1 oz or so, cut off a large block, per person.'

PRUDENCE HEADEY

'When the Second World War broke out, being exempted from military service, I got a job filling sandbags at the Corporation Yard down Newnham Avenue. These sandbags were placed all around the town to protect buildings of importance, such as the Town Hall, Shire Hall, and so on. Another of my war-time jobs was at the Water Works in

Manton Lane where the sand had to be scraped off the filter beds, wheeled up to the big heap to be washed, and then put back again.

You weren't supposed to leave a job during the war time, and you had to go before a tribunal to get permission. I got permission to leave the Water Works to work at Simplex Locomotives and Dumpers. They made equipment for use on the gun turrets of the tanks; it was all war work that they did.

I later applied for a job at Cardington Aerodrome where I worked as a fitter's mate. Whilst I was working at Cardington many balloons were being cut up but some were still in use. We put new bearings in the winches where the balloons were attached. These were the barrage balloons which were placed over towns in Britain so enemy planes couldn't fly over. There were wires hanging down from them, and this stopped the aircraft bombing certain buildings. They were possibly being dismantled because radar had been developed, or when Britain was getting the military advantage. This was the main industry at Cardington at that time, which was about half-way through the war, and then I left to go on the Labour Exchange, in 1943. They then sent me to do war work at W. H. Allens, Queens Works, Bedford, where I stayed for thirty-five years.

I was in the Civil Defence after the war and have a Long Service Medal from the Queen. I was a member of the St. John's Ambulance Brigade and a First Aid Worker at W. H. Allens, where I was employed as a Slinger. We had to attach slings to all the parts of machinery, for the fitter, and to the turbines and diesel engines and so on, so heavy equipment could be lifted when complete. It was marine engineering. War Ships built at that time were fitted with smoke screens and W. H. Allens supplied the blowers, ventilation fans and lighting sets: much of their work was for the Admiralty. They also made equipment such as turbines and diesel lighting sets for ferries, and liners including the Oriana.

Once the Bedford prison was bombed and there was an attempt to bomb W. H. Allens and the railway station. All the people had to go down the shelters. The bomb marks are still visible on the prison walls. Shelters were provided in the basement of properties in Bromham Road, just before the junction with Union Street, on the site of the recently-built flats.

When the Territorials were first called up they did their drills in Union Street. My brother Herbert was with them. His war-time experiences included Dunkirk, and he was later with the Desert Rats and fought in Italy.

All my brothers were in the Second World War. Herbert was with the Territorials, Douglas went to Burma in the Royal Engineers, and Alf was in the Royal Marines. He joined up at eighteen and was commissioned on the aircraft carrier Hermes for two years in China waters.

When my brother Alf was on the battle ship Duke of York, it took Churchill to America for a meeting. During gunnery practice on one occasion the crew that went before Alf's left a charge of gun-cotton in the gun. When the second crew came and put another charge of gun-cotton in it, it blew the gun up and killed three of the men. Alf, being a gun layer, was trapped in his seat, but had the presence of mind to put his mouth into a ventilation shaft to prevent being gassed. Nevertheless, he was very badly burnt and was in Bermuda Hospital for six months. He was later wounded four times and served on the Russian convoys.

Two of my brothers came home on leave at one time, and my mother wrote to the War Office to request that Alf be allowed to come at the same time, but he was in Russia then and could not be granted leave. Eventually, however, all four of us met together in Bedford Park, when I was in a bath chair with paralysis down my right side, after a road accident in 1937. They tipped me out – playfully – and told me to walk! We all enjoyed a fortnight's leave together.'

GEORGE BROWN

'I used to 'ave to go in the slaughter'ouse, and I 'ave to say it, I could kill a pig. I never ought to say it but during the war I was very popular at the SKF Co because I used to let 'em 'ave no end of pork when the rationing was on. That is a fact. I felt sorry for some people. When they 'ad these parties at Christmas they'd say, "Eric you'd do me a good turn if you'd do so and so", so I used to le 'em 'ave it. But I took a great chance 'cause some evenin's when I used to put it in me bags and that, and go to Luton with the stuff, if I'd been stopped I'd really 'av been caught out.

A fellow I used to let 'ave a lot o' pork, 'e used to keep a public 'ouse up 'itchin Road. I got on well with 'im because 'e used to let me 'ave plenty o' sugar you see. As luck 'd 'ave it, I got this sugar and I delivered the pork. So I went to see 'im about a week after and 'e says, "Ain't you been stopped outside?" I says, "No, why?" 'E says, "Well they raided me yesterday" – and I tell you 'ow it was done. There was a sergeant in charge of the meat for the army; 'e got 'old of a lot of lambs and 'ad 'em delivered in this place and they 'ad 'em down the cellar. 'E got friendly with a woman, this sergeant did, and 'e cut a big leg o' lamb off once and there was a bus stop just near this pub. It was a foggy night and 'e said to this woman "'ere y'are, 'ere's a big joint for ya. "Get going" 'e says, "don't ask questions". 'E got the wrong woman and she went to the police with this leg o' lamb. 'O course, they raided 'im and found all these lambs. They found pork and porks too. They didn't know where the pork came from but they found out where the lamb come from. The sergeant 'e got time and the landlord 'e 'ad to pay about £500 or £600.

Ya see, during the war there was a lot of things done like that, and there isn't anybody who can say they didn't 'ave things above what their ration was. Honestly.' ERIC THORNE

'During the Second World War I enlisted in Derbyshire and was then moved to Kirby Lonsdale in the Lake District. I was posted to Ireland, just outside Belfast, for three years until

February 1944. I finished up in Belgium where I was hospitalised. The War ended on 8 May 1945 in Europe and in August in the Far East. I was stationed outside Brussels and was in the Royal Army Service Corp and driving a truck. I stopped to pick up an American who said "It's all over buddy" and I just couldn't believe it.

I went into hospital the day after the Japanese capitulated, and was returned to Wales where I remained in hospital. I was demobbed in November 1945. After the war I worked at the Royal Aircraft Establishment in Bedford for five years, but gave it up to return to the farm. After a short period I resumed work at the RAE where I remained until my retirement. I spent twenty-two years there altogether and for this I receive a small pension, for which I am thankful.'

JOHN THORNE

'When my husband was called up for war service in 1942 I took over his job as insurance agent for the duration of the war. There was then National Insurance business to be attended to and there were many evacuees whose accounts had to be kept separately. I met many strange characters. One old man I remember particularly had been an East End docker. He was crippled with arthritis and unable to move at all. He and his wife and some members of his family were billeted in condemned small houses in Church Square, Bedford, where Woolworth was built when they were demolished. He used to tell me that if they had their back door open rats would come in and run along the mantlepiece. I never saw them myself so cannot confirm this. His wife was delighted to tell me that she had saved her best tea service when they had to leave their home after bombing and that she had it there with her in Bedford. What strange priorities people had!

When the Second World War started I had been living in Maulden for almost ten years. When the first air raid siren sounded everybody rushed outside – I don't quite know why!

Along came PC Holliman "Get indoors all you lot or I'll run the lot of you in", said he, and we all meekly obeyed! I shall never forget the night Coventry was bombed, the incessant drone of German bombers. We were lucky here in the village. I believe one bomb made a crater in a field. I heard at the time that it had disturbed some carrots! Carrots were very important in those days. Lorry loads of them were sent to market every day, along with other market garden produce – radishes, lettuces, onions, leeks, brussels sprouts, and the famous Maulden celery. Now the wonderful ground where all these were grown is mostly covered by houses and we are often obliged to buy imported things which are not comparable in quality or flavour.

There were a few bombs in the outlying woods and I remember a raid in Bedford one morning when my children were at school in Bedford, and there were several casualties. On the whole life had to go on as usual as far as possible but it was a time of terrible stress and strain even for us here in the country. I hope and pray that young mums will never have to face up to anything like it again. I watched the first batch of evacuee children from London arriving at the Midland Road station in Bedford with their gas masks and pathetic bags and bundles of possessions. They looked so forlorn. I just stood and cried. We shall never be able to assess what happened to the lives and minds of those children and their parents.

School life was difficult too. At one school I had to take the children into a brick shelter when the siren went. It was lit by candles and very damp and cold. At another children and staff were all herded into one big classroom which was permanently blackened out. Then one of our evacuee teachers played the piano and we were all supposed to sing. Singing was the last thing I felt like – my mind was far away. Looking back, I am still quite unable to see the wisdom of herding us all together.

I think of the Maulden lads who served in the army and

other services. Bill Eddy and Cliff Roberts perished. Bill Griffiths was a prisoner of the Japanese but he survived and is still around, living in Ampthill. I remember him well as a little boy with a truck on wheels, doing errands for his mother.

Frank Blackaby, an old boy of Bedford Modern School, took part in the Berlin Air Lift. He has long since left the village. Ray Herman was in the army from 1940–1946 and was at the battle of Monte Cassino in Italy. He is now retired and takes his part in village life. Norman Keens was in the Parachute Regiment. He was captured at Arnham and held prisoner by the Germans until the end of hostilities.

I watched Fred Kirby go off after embarkation leave in 1943, carrying heavy kit. His father, who had served in the First World War, and who suffered ever after from the effects of gas, accompanied him to the bus stop. Fred served in Sicily, North Africa and Italy. He died on September 26, 1988, and is remembered with affection and respect in the village. He leaves a younger sister, Betty, to whom he was very attached, and a brother, Geoff, who keeps his corner of "The Knoll" so attractive.

Fred Chappell, who contributes to our magazine from time to time, served in North Africa and many other countries. Stan Jones, who provides some illustrations for the magazine, served in the Royal Navy. I remember he used to illustrate his letters home to his wife and children during his war service. Two brothers, Frank and Herbert Fisher were in the services, Frank in the army and later a prisoner of war in the East. Herbert was in the navy. Their mother used to tell me about them and ask for news of a young relative of mine who was sent on a special mission after Singapore and never seen again. There must have been other servicemen whom I cannot immediately call to mind.

I recall two Maulden girls who served in the WRAF. Betty Cherry (now Mrs Spreadborough) was one. She still lives in Maulden. The other was Connie Abbot. I cannot recall her married name. *Audrey Sinfield served in the ATS. She has lived in the United States of America (Louisiana) for many years. Marion Kirby and her sister Doreen did ambulance work. Marion has also lived in America for some years. Doreen (now Mrs Fleet) lives in Ampthill.'*

GLADYS WALLIS

'My husband was a prisoner for four years in a Japanese prisoner of war camp during the last war, and was very ill when he came home. He suffered from tropical diseases and had severe headaches.'

MARY JEFFS

'During the Second World War my husband was working on the barrage balloons, and was posted at Cardington and Walthamstow, but not abroad. I think he was more scared than I was. While we were living in Stanmore, I slept in a Morrison shelter which was like a big table with wire round the bottom, and which was in the lounge. There were

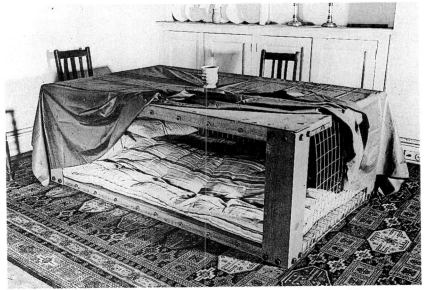

Morrison Shelter. Photo: courtesy The Imperial War Museum.

Anderson shelters which were dug-outs, and some people slept in those. I had a window blown out by a doodlebug that came over, and that was bad enough. For the duration of the war, I was living in London, where we had our own house.

I had to do war work because I had no children, and was in the Stores at the London Aircraft Protection factory where the Halifax Bombers were manufactured. Nightwork there was 7.30pm to 7.30am, and I hated it but the alternative was fire watching which I thought was worse. The factory was near Elstree, and I believe buses are repaired there now. I was put in charge of Stores, and issues, and wasn't familiar with this kind of work. When asked – whilst still new to the organisation – for a rat-tail file I wrote on the requisition 'rat-tale' and this led to a considerable amount of leg-pulling for some time afterwards. It was quite a large concern, employing about two thousand people.'

SARAH HILLS

'I was in the St. John's Ambulance Brigade for twenty-five years, at Stewartby [London Brick Co] and then at Kempston, and only left the Brigade in 1954 when I was diagnosed as

Football team at North Allerton. Stan fourth from left, standing.

Stan at North Allerton.

having a brain tumour. I received my medical training in Sidmouth, Devon, and was a male nurse with the RAF at Weeton near Blackpool and then at North Allerton, until I was demobbed. I helped to set it up, in North Allerton, and was there when the first patient arrived. It was like a general hospital for the Air Force. I chose this career course with the RAF because of my experience in the St. John's Ambulance Brigade you see.'

STANLEY LOVELL

'During the war years with the food shortages and rationing, there were government incentives to encourage pig breeding. Food vouchers could be obtained in exchange for the provision of an agreed quantity of pork to the Food Office. About ten local people had this facility to produce pigs, and the Food Office arranged the collection of the animals and their transportation to Wiltshire for slaughter.

I had two brothers who served in the Second World War and they were both fortunate in escaping serious injury and

L–R: Connie's brother, Percy, Geoff Mepham, younger son of Wootton Primary School Head (William Mepham), and Albert Gilbert, local historian.

returned safely home, but I remember others who were less fortunate.

I am proud to have been associated with the War Savings Campaign 1944, and at having been awarded a Certificate of Honour for my part in encouraging savings through the Wootton WVS, as a part of the Wings for Victory National Savings Campaign 1943. The Wootton WVS Savings Group raised almost £9,000 and my role in this was to sell savings stamps and issue the certificates. I also received a special message of congratulations from the Queen, which is one of my most treasured possessions.'

CONSTANCE ROBINSON

'As war seemed inevitable in 1938, preparations were made by the Government, and I was engaged by the local council as registration officer to go around the village of Thurleigh and issue to each person a National Registration Card. It took several days to cover the whole of the village, a bicycle being the chief means of transport.I started off by giving myself the first card, my code numbers and letters being D.Q.I-I. A sigh of relief came when Mr Neville Chamberlain visited Herr Hitler and on his return produced a document signed by Herr Hitler himself pledging that Germany would not go to war with England again. But peace lasted only for another twelve months.

Work dropped off again as people with thatched roofs thought they would be burnt down with Hitler's incendiary bombs. This theory proved to be wrong as, when the bombs fell on tiles or slated roofs, they penetrated through to the bedrooms below setting fire to the house, but with the thatched roof they bounced off to burn out on the ground below.

Again it seemed that every able-bodied man was called up for the services and that made a shortage of labour again. This time I managed to get a job with the Council helping to widen the very narrow roads through the village. The war had been on for about eight months when work started on building an airfield near the village of Thurleigh, hence the widening of the roads to accommodate the heavy lorries loaded with sand, gravel, cement and other materials for this purpose. When construction of the airfield was completed, the Royal Air Force moved in; after a few months a squadron of the Polish Air Force took over; and sometime in 1942 the American 8th Army Air Force arrived, bringing with them squadrons of large four-engined "Flying Fortress" bombers. The village soon became alive with American service men. Quite a number of the village girls were married to these Service people and after the war returned to America to join their husbands.'

WALTER 'REG' PARROTT

'During the depression and war time, people used to queue for coal and coke along Prebend Street in Bedford. Many would collect it in old prams. I have queued there myself. From 1942 people could only get extra coal if they had a new baby.

I used to swap flour, sweet and other coupons with friends, in order to get what I needed. I remember being on the Bedford market at six o'clock in the morning in the hope of getting a cake.'

FREDA BROWN

'I was in the Red Cross for years. During the Second World War we had a First Aid post locally which had to be manned at weekends. At one time life for us wasn't worth living, as every time the warning sounded we had to turn out, and this happened frequently. Going backwards and forwards to the First Aid post put us at risk too, and there were complaints about it, and so eventually we were each given special hours for manning the post, which was much better.

There were two courses that we had to take, First Aid and Home Nursing, and we had to qualify in both. During the war we were trained for treatment in the case of chemical warfare and I won the cup for Bedfordshire in this. There was a competition and I got the most marks. We had to fit gas masks and I removed a pair of glasses when fitting one, as I did with my own glasses. This won me extra marks!

There was only one casualty in Dunstable during the Second World War, as I recall, and he was not seriously injured. He was injured in the arm by shattered glass when some bombs were released in the area.

We used to have to go to the Luton and Dunstable Hospital and work in different departments. We dressed up the same as everyone else, and I remember being asked to tie one doctor's apron in the operating theatre. I then had to watch while the operation was carried out.

There were many bombs which fell around Whipsnade, and we couldn't understand at the time why they were bombing the zoo. We later discovered that Bomber Command Headquarters were nearby! The Germans knew this but we didn't.'

ELSIE ENGLAND

'So many things were in short supply during the war, and as for bathing, we were only allowed to have x number of inches in the bath and children needed a bath every night, so the neighbours got together and drew a bath-full of water and we took it in turns, in first one house and then another. Boys and girls shared the same water. We could boast later, about the many people we'd had a bath with. We had a tank on the wall which was switched on to heat up the water at bath-time. We had no central heating, just one fire in the sitting room and upstairs lino and a rug by the bed. We were tough. Vests, liberty bodices (white, with wide shoulder straps, hip length with suspenders), woolly hand-knitted stockings in the winter, for school, and long navy blue knickers with elastic in the legs and pocket in the front, and hand-knitted ribbed skirts stitched on to the top half of a petticoat and a matching jumper to go over the top. Hand-knitted gloves and scarves, *hand-knitted swimsuits in the summer. They stretched and sagged when they got wet and you were full of gritty sand between your legs!*

A friend of my mother's sent a parcel of clothes over at one time, from Australia, and I acquired a navy blue blazer with gold braid trimming. I used to wear it to the tennis club, and was proud to be seen in it.

Petrol was rationed but you could get a private hire car. Father had a holiday in Jaywick about 1944, on the doctor's orders. We took small tins of corned beef and packets of lard, which he used for baking his pasties. No money changed hands: we got petrol by exchanging the tins of corned beef. We had a tinned-roof bungalow at Jaywick and on the day we left there was a thunder storm and the whole roof leaked. That was my first sight of the seaside, the first time I had ice cream, which came in a greaseproof paper packet, like a little brickett.

I don't think fruit and vegetables were on ration but the supply rationed them. Boats arrived infrequently. The doctor said I had to have vitamin C orange juice and mother had a special form to get oranges when they were in. I never tasted banana until the late 1940s. We got dried bananas but they weren't like the real thing. The corned beef came from the Argentine (and still does). Rose-hip syrup, orange juice and cod-liver oil were prescribed for every child.

Even the family doctor, Dr Heggarty, had to be paid for if he came, but we didn't pay – he had fillet steak instead!

One of our neighbours had a Morrison shelter and we used to have children's tea parties and birthday parties around it, using it as a table. We'd have sandwiches, fairy cakes if we were lucky, with mock icing, and tinned fruit.

After the war we had a big street party. Our piano was put outside, the shop was used for storing the food before the party, I was dressed as a pierrot and father dressed up as a clown. That was an occasion to remember!'

PRUDENCE HEADEY

ARP and Home Guard

'During the "War Years" the Hall (Moggerhanger Village Hall) was used for ARP activities and for a great number of other functions, designed to help the war effort and also to lessen the tensions that build up on such occasions, such as entertaining the troops with dances, bingo sessions, whist drives, tea parties and inviting visitors from the surrounding villages. One group of Airforce personnel came from the RAF Station at Tempsford from whence Whitley, Lysander and Halifax Aircraft transported British Secret Service Agents and stores for Allied Resistance Groups in enemy occupied Europe. Interesting items in the "Stores" were razor blades that could be used as very good compasses and maps drawn on silk handkerchiefs for use by prisoners of war during their attempts to escape to the Allied Lines.

A "Service Committee" was formed by Mesdames Whiteman, Dean and Phillips and Messrs F. Hall, Braybrook, F. Randall, H. Reid and G. Whiteman to send "Comforts" such as socks, scarves and cigarettes to men serving in HM Forces. It is also said that Mrs O. Dean was a member of the First Aid Team and that her duties included driving a horse and cart to Sandy and Blunham railway stations.

To counteract the effect of bombs dropped by enemy aircraft Moggerhanger, like every other place in the land, provided a Civil Defence Organisation with its Headquarters at Village Farm.

F. W. Matthews was Chairman and Food Officer

Brig. Gen. W. B. Thornton was Vice Chairman

L. V. Davison represented Moggerhanger Home Guard

W. C. Hill and G. E. Braybrook were Senior ARP Wardens

F. E. Hall and L. Hill were Special Constables

P. Pitts and F. Frith represented National Fire Service

Mrs Hales (First Aid Point)

It was noted that three "Wells" were still functioning and could be used as an emergency water supply. Twenty-one men had volunteered to fill in bomb craters. There were 29 picks,

30 axes, 149 shovels, 22 crowbars, 27 wheelbarrows, 20 tree-felling saws, 28 ladders, 8 water tanks, 22 stirrup pumps, 26 ropes, 150 sandbags, 145 buckets and 4 water-carts that could be used if it became necessary. In the ARP Centre (Village Hall) there were 1 stretcher, 66 mattresses and 132 blankets.'

H. S. BROWN

'My youngest brother joined up for the Second World War. Every male aged between eighteen and forty-one was supposed to be registered but some occupations were exempted, including farming. People still had to register but were exempt from service. One brother was in the ARP (Air Raid Precautions) and the rest in the Home Guard. We worked all day and trained all night. It was not silliness and fun, as portrayed in Dad's Army. *There were three patrols. I patrolled the railway line from Oakley to Newton Blossomville each evening. We were stationed at Turvey. There were two hours of summertime then, not one. It was light until 11pm. I was up at 5am milking cows. In the first place I had one night on Home Guard and also Sunday mornings. I worked first thing on Sunday on the farm, and then went on to train. Later we had to attend First Aid Classes in Bedford on two evenings. We also attended Gas Classes on another evening, and were taught about the different gases, what precautions*

Horace Welch in the Home Guard, pictured at the back of their yard in Wick End, Stagsden.

to take, antidotes and treatment. There was a gas chamber at Bromham Hospital which was used in these exercises. It got very busy towards the end.

My young brother came through the conflict, and was serving in Germany when the war finished.'

HORACE WELCH

'In 1940 the 2nd Bedfordshire Battalion of the Home Guard was formed and was commanded by Lieutenant Colonel the Hon. M. C. H. Bowes-Lyon who had for his second I/C Colonel G. H. Wells. Men from Moggerhanger, Blunham and Northill joined the Home Guard and they became "B" Company commanded by Brig. Gen. W. B. Thornton, DSO, JP, and his Platoon Commanders were Lieuts. L. V. Davison (Moggerhanger), W. H. Rose (Blunham) and F. Vincent (Northill). Members of the Home Guard did two parades per week when they were given instruction about such weapons as Rifles, Tommy guns, Sten guns, Lewis gun, Browning machine gun, Solothurn AA machine gun, Northover projector, Spigot mortar, Smith gun, revolvers of various design, grenade throwers, the Sticky Bomb, land mines and a "Bomb on a little wooden truck". (Details about these "Bombs" were not recorded.) The main duties of the Home Guard were to provide security for Railway Stations, Tunnels, Waterworks, Electric Power Stations, Gas Works, Ammunition Factories and to keep a good look out for enemy agents being dropped by parachute.'

H. S. BROWN

'During the war I was in the ARP (before the formation of the Home Guard). I then left to join the Home Guard, where I had the task of forming a commander squad. I have pleasant recollections of the Army School of Physical Training on Dunstable Downs – jolly good food there, better than at home! I was assigned guard duties to safeguard the railway lines during the Normandy landings. The men manned a

lookout post each night to make sure there were no parachute drops.'

ARTHUR 'LOL' THEW

'My father's shop was the local ARP post after dark and they congregated there for fire watching. On one occasion someone wrote in the diary "only the moon looked down tonight"!'

PRUDENCE HEADEY

Evacuees

'We had the evacuees during the Second World War, and this made the class so big. They were full up at Tennyson Road [Luton], and we had to take ten more. The parents were not too pleased about it but when it was time for the children to go back, they didn't want them to go. They were very nice children.

I also helped with the billeting of the evacuees.'

HILDA PUDDEPHATT

'Just before the outbreak of war in 1939 mass evacuation of children from London and other important cities and towns took place, being distributed to towns and villages thought less likely to be bombed. It was at this time that I was chosen to be the billeting officer for the village of Thurleigh. About two or three days before the war started several bus loads of men, women and children arrived at the village school, which was the distribution centre. They turned out to be a whole catholic school of about a hundred souls in all, including school masters and two nuns. With my small clerical staff and the help of my wife and the village constable, also members of the local scout troop acting as guides, all these people were in their respective billets by nightfall.

Each weekend some of the parents would make the journey from London to visit their children and some of the latter who couldn't settle down returned home with their parents.

The next party to arrive were from Newhaven. The people being more used to the country, settled in very well and stayed until the end of the war. Many friends were made and after they returned home, many people from Thurleigh were invited to Newhaven for holidays. Many of the children are now married with children of their own, and occasionally still make a visit to the village to see old friends.'

WALTER 'REG' PARROTT

'During the Second World War and with the large-scale evacuation, many diseases were spread particularly among children. People used to get red mites under the skin, and there was dermatitis, impetigo, consumption, diptheria, and bed-wetting, caused as much through emotional stress as anything else no doubt. It was common for children to be scrubbed down.'

FREDA BROWN

'Evacuees came to Luton in large numbers. The first thing mother did was tell them they were having a bath. When we took in evacuees my sister and I slept in the same room in a double bed, which caused aggravation. We ended up with a bolster between us. We had an army sergeant's son living with us at one time, Lesley Clinch. His wife had died and mother took the boy in for a year or so. He was a teenager and went to Luton Grammar School, but was a little horror. He liked to do "operations" on my sister and I, until my mother discovered what was going on! There were a coach-load of children arrived in our street one evening. They were paraded up and down the road until they had all found a home. They all had a label on them and their little bags. We took in two little girls but I don't remember them being with us for long. Possibly their mother took them back. Those children looked terrified when they arrived.'

PRUDENCE HEADEY

Prisoners of War

'When the threshing machine arrived at the farm and my uncle needed additional help, about eight prisoners would come from the camp but apart from an extra busy time like this only two came to work regularly. One of these men was a sailor in the Kaiserlich Marine, the other fellow was a soldier, one of the Prussian Guard, both very strong and powerful men. Whilst escorting these men to and from the camp (a distance of approximately three miles), we walked mainly by footpath across fields, and en route we had to cross the river by a footbridge. these men could easily have picked me up and thrown me into the river, but we were on very good terms with each other.'

WALTER 'REG' PARROTT

'In 1945 I was invalided out of the airforce. I was taken on at the brickworks as a chargehand. They had prisoners of war working there then – brought by lorry load from Clapham – three or four lorry loads of Germans. Each man was supposed to make so many bricks, and there were four setters to a kiln, with an Englishman. They were real good workers, very efficient, those Germans, trained to the hilt, real good workmen. After they went back we had the EVWs – European Voluntary Workers – refugees from Poland and from other east European states, who replaced the repatriated Germans. They had to be taught the job, but they turned out good men. There was a camp at the Elstow Storage Depot and another at Marston, built to accommodate the foreign workers. The POWs also worked at the Liddlington and Ridgemont brickworks and there was a POW camp at Green Lane in Clapham. I believe the buildings are still there, and are now used by a fencing contractor.

When that labour force [London Brick] began to dry up, as many got jobs elsewhere, the company turned to Southern Italy for labour, in the early 1950s. There was never any immigrant labour before the war. Many of these people live in Bedford nowadays.'

STANLEY LOVELL

'I was stationed at Colmworth in 1945, where there was a prisoner of war camp, all Germans. These Germans were mainly allowed out on day work. Many were camp-based but billeted out with farmers. It was my task to tend to their welfare. Some were ill and in hospital: I kept track of them and dealt with rations to farmers. We're talking about several thousand men.

The photographs I have were taken in the camp canteen, I think. Not many British were allowed in the compound in case they fraternised. When the men put on a concert they produced all the decorations, props and garments themselves, and the front of the stage they made in cast concrete. They made their own instruments and sang beautifully. They were very musical. The audience were other prisoners and British staff. It was all very entertaining. I don't know how they shaved their legs or where they got their tights from! The prisoners ran their own affairs through their Camp Commandant, who ran the camp on their behalf. Any serious charges were referred to the Camp Adjutant.

In some camps there were problems with the Italians and

A performance staged by German prisoners of war.

69

girls. The Germans were very orderly. It made me ashamed to type out some of their confessions!

At Tempsford they formed an orchestra and they were good. There were four violins. Classical stuff, not jazz, and played from memory as they had no music. Mozart was a favourite, of course. I've got a picture of the orchestra taken at Everton Camp, One person in the picture was my batman, the fat one I believe. He was very good. He was one of the cooks: this was his main duty. The Everton Camp was a smaller one, hundreds rather than thousands of prisoners. British staff numbered roughly six at Everton whereas at Colmworth there were about thirty.

The prisoners were repatriated in stages, depending on their status. If they were SS they didn't stand much chance of early repatriation. Factors were age, domestic circumstances back home, length of time in captivity. The evaluation was done from the War Office. We sent their records up by rail and these records were accompanied by an armed guard. They contained statements they made when captured and the results of interrogation.

I was in Colmworth for a year before being moved to Everton and the Sandy area, and finally finished up outside Sheffield, at a camp called Lodgemore, in West Yorkshire, where we were snow-bound for a fortnight at one time. I was demobbed from there.

One incident at Sheffield I recall. I was responsible for the documentation and had an office with about twelve German clerks who handled their own mail and finances because they were paid in token money. I left that to them and they were no problem at all. In the evenings when the day's routine was over I would go back in the office to use the typewriter to write letters home and I was there one evening typing away and one of the staff in the office came back to use the typewriter for the same reason, but had with him a parcel from his wife in Germany. I was there when he opened it and burst into tears. I went and sat beside him and put my arm around his shoulder and discovered that the parcel contained six rock cakes made with black flour, and they were as hard as ever I had seen: you couldn't eat them. He cried because he knew what his wife had foregone to make and send these buns. We cried together! We corresponded for two or three years after the war and I discovered he was a Christian, so we had something in common.

There was no hot water in the nissan hut but there was a tank on the rafters and if you wanted a shower it was a cold one. A chap called "Blondie" did the barbering. He's fourth from left in the photograph of the drama production. We conversed in a mixture of French, English and German. It was quite hilarious.

As I was a conscientious objector, when I was drafted into the army I was put in the NCC Non-combatant Corp. Most of us after training were assigned to clerical or other non-combatant duties. I was given clerical work in the orderly room at Colmworth. We weren't allowed to have promotion: we started and finished as privates. It was that or prison! The person I worked with was the equivalent of orderly room

Another dramatic production at the POW camp.

sergeant. We had our privileges, and I virtually had a private batman. We had private quarters but there was one officer and myself. The others slept in common dormitories. I had the privileges of an officer because I am a Christian, but not their pay, which was a bone of contention with some of the NCOs. 3/- a day [three shillings], and if we saved anything the wives wanted it! I think I can say I was completely broke at the end of the war.

The men used the money in the camp shop on toiletries, sweets, etc. Our business with them was done in the cigarette trade: we could buy them at a cheap rate at the NAFE. If they did anything for us we paid them in cigarettes. I have an attaché case still which one of them made for me with tools borrowed from farmers, hand-made, all made in wood, with dove-tailed corners. I cannot remember how many cigarettes I gave for it.'

STAN JOSLIN, FEERING, ESSEX

The GIs

During the Second World War Bedfordshire saw the arrival of the American Eighth Air Force. There were seven Eighth

A double GI wedding, believed to be in Milton Ernest.

Air Force bases with three-and-a-half thousand men on each base at any one time. The inhabitants of the county's tiny villages were overwhelmed, not least the young girls. The GIs had charm, and money, were sociable and through their bases, could obtain many of the things in abundance which were in short supply in this country.

Of the 144 Bedfordshire girls who became GI brides, six came from the village of Milton Ernest.

'I was still at school when the Americans arrived. One morning the village [Milton Ernest] woke to the sounds of Americans at Milton Ernest Hall. You can imagine what an impact this had on all of us.

The Americans gave the villagers chocolate, sweets and things they couldn't have otherwise got, and we were grateful to them. My friend and I just wanted to get home after school and dress up in things we'd got from the jumble sales, so as to look older. We cadged lipsticks off the older girls and reached with our finger down the tube to scrape out what little was left. We'd go down and stand on the corner of the road and wait for the trucks to come at night, taking these guys to Bedford, on their nights off. They'd shout "Hi honey. Have you got an older sister", much to our disappointment. We thought they would be after us! They'd throw us chocolate bars and chewing gum. They made such an impact on us, because we had nothing in the village. My dad was an ordinary farm worker earning 12/6d a week.

My mother did washing for the Americans and there was no washing machine and electric iron in those days. There was a communal copper in the wash-house at the back. My mum earned extra shillings washing, which she did one day a week. The American who brought the washing to her was nineteen and I was in love with him. I used to tell all the girls I had an American boyfriend. I hasten to say he was not in love with me! This particular night he brought the washing and asked my mum to do it a bit special. Mum used a flat iron, and rubbed in candle grease to iron in the pleats. He asked to take me to a dance – he thought I was sixteen. I went, but my mother didn't know. She had gone to see her friend. My friend and her boyfriend got me in.

James 'Scotty' McPhail.

Connie, aged thirteen.

My American "boyfriend" was a photographer and I still have a photograph which he took of me when I was thirteen. I've also got a photograph of him. He was called "Scotty" but his name was James McPhail. I have tried to trace him in recent years, but with no success. It was because he took me to a dance at Milton Ernest Hall that I met and shook hands with Glen Miller, as he was based there when he came to entertain the servicemen.

Six girls from the village married GIs and left for the States. I know that three of them have now passed away, but the others still return to visit relatives. Not all of the GI brides remained in America. Some of them went back to shacks in the woods! It wasn't as good, romantic and glamorous as they had imagined.

At Midland Road Station en route for America.

Dancing the night away.

There were girls who became pregnant. It was a terrible thing if you were a village girl and got pregnant. You just didn't talk about it. There was a home for unmarried mothers by the cemetery in Bedford. Naturally parents were worried about their daughters. Condoms were about, but rarely used and not easily obtainable. We were so ignorant at that time, that we actually thought you mustn't kiss or you might have a baby! I had to be home early.

One day dad came home and said to mum "I've met an old Yank who wants a bicycle and said he'd give me a ten bob note if I got him one". Mum said "You need your bicycle to get to work". Anyhow, we had barns around the back of the house and for four nights dad disappeared around the barn, even though there was a blackout in force. I might say that even the toilets – the bucket toilets – were around the back too. I used to be frightened to go out there in the dark. Anyhow, I went out and found dad painting a bike. He said to mum "I'm just going down the pub mate: I'll be back soon", returning at nine o'clock looking pleased with himself. "There you are my duck" he said to mum, "there's five shillings for you and five for me". He'd only pinched his neighbour's old bike, painted it and put a bell on it! He was always thoughtful towards mum though, and even in the last days of her life he'd go to the pub and bring her back a Guinness and packet of crisps before he'd have his drink.

The Americans had money, were brash and good-looking, and it seemed to me at the time that these men had stepped off the movie screen. They looked wonderful. They did so much for us. We couldn't get ice-cream but they got it for us, by taking it to 30,000 feet in the B15s, to freeze it for our parties. You've heard that saying that they were "over-paid, over-sexed and over here". Well, they weren't over-paid: the fact is that our soldiers were under-paid. These young Americans were told they were coming to England to die and would never return to the States. I was nearly fourteen when they left, and the majority of them had gone by 1945. Quite a lot of them chose to remain in this country.

Over the years I've become very interested in this part of our history, and both my husband and I are Eighth Airforce Historians. I personally have done a tremendous amount of research, and have set up a museum in my own home, which I hope one day will transfer into the town of Bedford.

I have contacted many of the GIs who served here during the war, and have entertained and assisted them when they, their children and their grandchildren have visited Bedfordshire. I've helped to put many people in touch, kept alive the memory of this important association, and in doing so, helped to foster Anglo-American relations. This is my hobby, my main interest, and my life. If I had as many pounds as I've had Americans in this house I would be a rich woman!

Each year on the last Sunday in May or the First in June, I attend the Memorial Day service at the Cambridge cemetery, where many of those Americans who lost their lives, are interred. Forty-nine servicemen from Thurleigh are buried there and we take forty-nine posies to lay on the graves. There are many touching and human stories connected with this period, and one was revealed to me through my contact with the cemetery.

When we laid the posies, we noticed year after year, a most beautiful bouquet of flowers on one particular grave. No-one knew where they came from, until someone contacted me through my association with the Eighth Air Force Historical Society, asking if I had a photograph of Michael Roscovich, known as the "mad Russian", who had been stationed at Thurleigh and was killed on 4 February 1944. It so happened that I did have a photograph of him.

I then discovered that the person who had left the bouquet and who contacted me was called Mary. She had met and fallen in love with Michael when he was stationed in Thurleigh, and had become pregnant and given birth to a son whom she called David. She subsequently married at the age of seventeen, and her husband, who was in the RAF, thought the child was his. It was not until after her third marriage, and forty-two years later, that she revealed to her son the identity of his natural father. She sends flowers to the grave regularly, and visits occasionally.

I met her at the Cambridge cemetery, with her grandsons, who bore a striking resemblance to the GI in my photograph. Mary was distraught, at her son's anger over the deception. Mary looked at the photograph which I handed to her and burst into tears, and said to the boys "there's your grandfather". She and I became great friends and her son was subsequently invited to lay the wreath on behalf of his father.

About four or five months later Mary was eager to contact any member of Michael's family and she and I met at the

Lt. Vail and the crew of 'Shoo Shoo Baby'.

cemetery again whilst I was escorting another group – we met quite by chance. Mary was feeling very stressed about David and said she had asked Michael for a sign that she did the right thing in telling David about him. When I got home that night, quite late, the telephone rang and an American announced that he was Chuck Roscovich, Michael's brother. He had read the newspaper that day and learned of my involvement with the veterans, and had seen my notice asking for any of Michael's relatives to contact me. He had obtained my phone number from the newspaper and phoned straight away. Bearing in mind the six-hour time difference, this must have happened about the time of Mary's visit to the grave! Was this the sign for which she'd asked? By another strange coincidence, he was married and had a son called David! And so Mary and David were put in touch with their relatives in America.'

CONNIE RICHARDS

'There were quite a number of GI brides from this parish, as Thurleigh was the headquarters of the American Army 306 Bombardment Group. There were two thousand American servicemen in the village [Thurleigh] at one time, but there was never any danger to the women.'

FREDERICK WILDMAN

'Podington was the local wartime aerodrome and I formed two lasting friendships there, with Limey and Derman Chuck, American GIs. Chuck was marrying the daughter of the publican in Odell, and we had a stag night before the wedding day, when Limey was sick upstairs. The following morning we blamed Chuck, who'd been stoned out of his mind, and who, possessed of guilt, cleaned up all the mess before his wedding! We had our good times as well as bad ones.'

ARTHUR THEW

The GI Bride

Mame Kotulka, a GI bride, whose family now live in Bedfordshire, met her husband whilst living in Scotland.

'When I look back on it now I really don't know how I ever did it, leaving a family I loved and a country I loved. At times here people ask me how was I able to do what I did, and I wonder, and then I feel like crying.

Yes, I am a GI war bride, and it sure is amazing what love can do. Joe, my husband, was in the American Army. I lived in Glasgow then, with my family, for six years of the war. Joe had arrived by ship to the Helensburgh, Gourock area, and lots of soldiers were sent to a place near us, a large institution, and from there were sent to their units. A girlfriend and myself were on our way to the movies, and at first seeing the soldiers we thought they were German prisoners. There was a high wall all round the building, and as we walked, soldiers were sticking their heads over, and we realised they were Americans. My friend and I stopped to talk, and that is how I met Joe: the date was August 26th, 1942. We made a date for the next day, a Sunday, and there was not much to do then in Scotland on a Sunday but go for a walk, and who did we meet but my parents, in their Sunday best, also taking a walk, and I guess seeing what I was up to! The next day Joe was on his way to England, but he wrote me.

Joe came to visit New Year's Eve, but I didn't know 'till later that he would be sailing for North Africa. I was only sixteen, almost seventeen, when I met Joe and he was twenty-three. We wrote each other and Christmas 1943 Joe was back, he came for a visit and wanted to get married, but my dad would only say OK for us to get engaged. Joe was determined and with my dad's consent we were married on October 2nd, 1944 in Lichfield, England. With D-day fighting going on, leave was hard to get. My mum and dad, my brother Jack and wife and my dad's cousin were there. My dad's aunt had moved in to take care of the family in Scotland.

We had a lovely wedding in a small chapel in the camp "Whittington Barracks", about four miles from Lichfield. The Army did most of it, and it was great, and we had a reception later in a Lichfield tea room, and after that off to the King's Arms. My mum and dad had a ball and made a week of it. Joe is Catholic and I am Presbyterian, and the ceremony was performed by a Catholic Priest, assisted by an American Army Chaplain.

Before getting married Joe and I had a lot of papers to fill out, and enquiries were made of course on both of us, and I had to go for an interview, and it was an American Army Chaplain who talked to me.

Joe had been lucky, he had gotten into a motor pool and he stayed in England. He had gone through North Africa and Sicily, earlier. In August 1945 Joe was sent to France to prepare for home, but it was October 1945 before he made it, and after a leave he was discharged from the Army on October 14th. I was pregnant and our son Joe was born October 10th, 1945.

Now the long wait started, but I was having second thoughts. I loved my mum and dad and brothers and sisters. My brother Jack was in the Air Force, George in the Army, Herb and Donald fifteen and twelve, Maggie and Doris eight and two-and-a-half. I was especially close to Doris. My mum was forty-three when Doris was born, and felt she was too old. I would take Doris with me whenever I could, and on a visit to me doctor for my pregnancy, he warned me that when I left home it was going to be hard to explain, and also hard for a two-year-old to understand where I had gone. Doris and our son Joe are two years apart and they had some fun together for six months but neither one remembers, but they have met since. Now I knew that one of these days I'd get my orders. If Joe had stayed in the Army, I would have been priority 1, as it was with a baby I was priority 2. My papers arrived one morning in April and I had thirty-six hours to get ready. Well that was it for me, and I told my mum, "I'm not going". She took a hold of me and said "You're going and you aren't crying either".

It sure was a busy thirty-six hours. My mum and dad, some family and friends, came to the train station. There were thirty-four brides going, and one had a bagpipe band seeing her off. We travelled all night to London, but right before we left, something that has always stayed with me, back then Scottish people found it hard to kiss and hug and say goodbye, and I'm on the train and looking at everyone, and all of a sudden the train shunted, and I screamed at the top of my lungs. I was told later that I gave everyone on the platform goose pimples. A young soldier, a brother of one of the brides, was a big help to all of us on that train journey south. We arrived at one station in London, and were taken by bus to another station and we were able to have a cup of tea there. My brother Jack arrived, my mum had sent him a telegram. He had an Air Force car and wanted to show me some of London. I hadn't known any of the Scottish brides, but I'd made a friend and she came along. We had been given a choice of trains for our next stop and 4pm was the last. Well Jack got tied up in some Air Force business and we spent most of the day in the car, and that was not much fun.

All the Scottish girls I travelled with went to Bournemouth and I went to Tidworth. The camp was just like being in the army, and we stayed twelve women in each area. Our names were on the beds. There were thirteen children in our area: one bride had two children. German prisoners did all the tasks, cleaning, cooking and so forth, and most of them were either older or very young. You could see that they really loved the children, and would watch them as we waited in line for our food.

The camp was difficult, everything so far apart and a lot of walking. My luggage was lost and I only had a few things for young Joe and myself, and I'd think to myself what have I gotten myself into! Leaving home and everyone had been awful, and I could cry now thinking about it.

Our first morning we had to attend a meeting in the Auditorium and were given our orders, and one was no fraternising with German prisoners, and anyone caught would be sent home. We were given physicals and briefings, and we'd go to the American Red Cross for some tea and cookies, and I met a nice lady from St. Louis and she found out that my luggage was lost and she gave me the things I needed. My luggage had actually gone on to Bournemouth, which I didn't know until I got on the ship, and then I returned what the Red Cross had given me, as I said I would.

Our travelling was very organised, the Army taking care of us wore special badges on their upper arm, a baby, diaper and safety pin on them. There was a place where we could do some washing and a drying room but things were stolen, so most of us washed our things near our own area and dried them the best we could. Each baby had a crib, but my Joe wasn't a happy camper, I guess he didn't know what he was missing, but he missed home too. We were awakened at 3am and told to get ready pronto for our trip to Southampton, that was by bus. I had no way to call my parents and I was just sick. Arriving at the docks in Southampton was just terrible. It was foggy and eerie and we could see the Queen Mary, she was in battleship grey and looked sad sitting there. We were put in pens, wooden fences in circles, some parents were there, and I am thinking what am I doing here! I was assigned to the wrong cabin but that was straightened out, the cabin was L-shaped and five brides, not all had babies. I had a top bunk and young Joe's cot was attached to the bottom bunk. It was deep, made of net and had a small mattress. A couple of girls and myself decided to walk about the Queen Mary to find out if she was as big as everyone said: this was before she sailed. We passed the telegraph office and there were telegrams posted on the outside and I'll never forget how I felt finding a telegram for me from my mum and dad, wishing me the best. That sure broke me up and does again right now. They must have kept in touch with everything and God bless them.

My luggage as I said was on the ship. We sailed and I said goodbye to Britain. I'm not a good sailor and needless to say after eating some of the goodies available, things we hadn't seen for years, I was sick, and we also hit a big storm and some of the upper decks were closed. We were going the Northern route, the Queen Mary had been given back to the UK and Canadian brides had priority. When we reached Nova Scotia it was snowing. In our cabin and I'm sure in all the others, there were names all over the walls. The Queen Mary had been used mostly for troop transport. Young Joe got so sick too, he had been raised on a milk formula and was now on a water-mixed one. Lots of babies were sick, and there were deaths. We had orders to be out of bed by a certain time and our bunks made up, but pretty soon too many were sick, and they brought us apples and saltine crackers to eat. We had more physicals, and the last one as we neared New York City and that was with a flash light. The one bride who was in the L part of our cabin was found to have lice and had to go to the hospital area.

There was some entertainment aboard the Queen Mary but hard to go to it with a baby and being sick. Taking a bath wasn't easy, it was salt water and wouldn't soap.

As we sailed past Long Island, the Immigration boarded and checked us out. When we docked we were told to get ready and organised, all information came over a loud-speaker, and then we had to listen for our names and that seemed to take forever. When mine was called I went towards the gang plank, a man spoke into what looked like a tube, if your husband was there you got off, and if not you stayed. I was told I could go down the gang plank and watch for my husband. A Red Cross lady met me at the bottom, and said I should let her have the baby. I didn't want to, but she insisted, and I knew he would cry. I didn't recognise my husband Joe, he had on a blue pinstripe suit and wore rimless glasses, and he sure looked different in civvies. He asked immediately where's the baby and needless to say the first time he saw his son, young Joe was screaming bloody murder. We landed May 10th, young Joe turned seven months that day and he had cut his first tooth. We had been on our way over two weeks.

Joe too had an experience, he had gone to New York City the day before, he was notified by the Red Cross when we were arriving. Back then there weren't the motels or hotels there are now. Joe had met some older dock workers and I guess he had told them why he was there. He was invited to go home with two of them and they were nice to him. He was lucky, it would be hard to do that today without being robbed or murdered.

With young Joe being sick we went to Joe's sister's home first, and the next day visited her doctor, and in a day or two young Joe was fine. We went to Joe's parents on May 12th which happened to be Mother's Day that year. We stayed with them about six months but it was hard for them and me. I don't think they had wanted Joe to marry overseas, but they themselves had come from Europe, his mum from Poland and dad from Slovakia just after 1900, and they had met in the USA. I guess all parents are protect-

Mame and baby Joe, with a niece, shortly after her arrival in America.

ive of their family. I was so homesick, and apartments then were hard to find, but life must go on and you make the best or the worst of it. Joe and I have survived, and we celebrated fifty years on October 2nd 1994, and now fifty-two years are on the way. Joe has had some health problems but is fine right now: he is seventy-six and I am seventy. We have a very nice family: Joe, Don, Gene and Darlene. We have four grandchildren and we also have four great-grandchildren and we are going to have another great-grandchild in May, so our family keeps getting bigger. Our family are all happy that Joe and I met, and it sure is amazing what love can do. I never dreamt when I was a child in Scotland that I would spend three-quarters of my life in the USA. I will be here fifty years this May 10th. So far I haven't become a citizen but I have been thinking lately that I might.

I didn't get back home for twenty-four years but I was lucky that my mum and dad and other family were able to come here, and I've been home again twice since.

It wasn't an easy thing to do leaving home and everyone, but it worked out, and I do hope that lots of the brides made it. I made friends with four of them in this area. I never joined the brides club and perhaps should have.'

MAME KOTULKA

The Women's Institute

Established in 1915 for the purpose of improving the quality of life for women generally but more especially women living in the countryside, the Women's Institute continued to be active throughout the war years. Providing information, promoting self-help, thrift, and home management for many women whose husbands were serving in the forces abroad or away from home, and organising fund-raising activities in support of the armed forces. The WIs promoted the well-being of women and their families by encouraging food production and food preservation, among other things, and just as importantly, provided an opportunity for women to meet, to form friendships, and be able to discuss everyday problems associated with coping alone in the difficult and prolonged period of the war.

The Wootton Women's Institute was one of very many throughout the country, actively engaged in educating and informing women through organised local events.

ABSTRACT FROM WOMEN'S INSTITUTE MINUTES FOR THE PERIOD 1941-1944

Ministry of Information Film Show dealing with the Army, Navy and Airforce

Scheme to help produce more vegetables *viz* onions and tomatoes

Bulk orders placed for preserving jars
Fruit preservation scheme
Competitions – best carrots, onions, potatoes

Talks on Wartime Gardening by Miss Wallis, Horticultural Department, Beds County Council

Gift Day Sale – proceeds to the 'boys of the village now serving with HM Forces' – for Xmas
Also presents sent to those on active service overseas and PO to those in Home Services. The three fallen were remembered in a wreath-laying ceremony at the War Memorial on December 24, 1942

Ministry of Information Films:
Aerial Activities
Fire Guard
Men and Machines
Sowing and Planting
Building for Victory

Whist Drive and social in aid of Warship Week. £12.0.0d raised towards purchase of three life saving jackets for HM Submarine 'Thorn'

Demonstration: Use of Remnants

Demonstration: Drying of Fruit, Vegetables and Herbs

Ministry of Information Films:
    ABCD of Health
    Wisdom of the Wild
    Men of Tomorrow
    Workers and War Front
    Paratroops
    Battle for Oil
('appreciative audience')

Cookery demonstration: Catering for Wartime

Letters received from members of HM Forces for Xmas presents. The list included 126 names (3 women)

Demonstration: Garment Reconstruction and Renovation

Demonstration: New from Old

Talk on reading the Meter and Simple Repairs (electric)

Wootton Wings for Victory Week

National Saving:
    WI Show and Handicrafts Exhibition 2.6.43 raised £5 and this was presented to the Wootton Wings for Victory committee

    Sale of Savings Certificates during the proceedings was £52.10s

Garden Meeting at Wootton House by kind permission of Col. and the Hon. Mrs Morgan-Grenville (1943)

Collection in aid of Prisoners of War Fund

Salute the Soldier day – Gift Day and Sale – stalls decorated in red, white and blue. Proceeds of £34 given to the Village Hall Fund and the Red Cross

Talk: 'How I have saved clothing coupons' – new from old theme

Xmas 1944: gifts to members of HM Forces. List now reached 176, five of whom are prisoners of war

Demonstration
on mending

President –
Sibyl Harriet
Monoux Doyne
Ditmus

Abstract from Wootton
WI Minutes
Courtesy President

Wootton War Memorial.

LEISURE AND ENTERTAINMENT

The ever-popular carousel.

The cakewalk.

LEISURE AND ENTERTAINMENT

Introduction

Prior to the days of radio and television, music hall and theatre were largely the haunts of the middle classes, whilst those of lesser means, and particularly those living in rural areas, found pleasure in the more simple things that life could offer, and in local entertainment, staged by amateurs. School entertainment, church social events, day-trips organised by the church or chapel, or by the 'local' [pub], the 'pictures', village fetes and visiting fairs and circuses, the parks, the garden and the allotment, walks, cycle rides and picnics: these are some of the ways in which ordinary country people amused themselves.

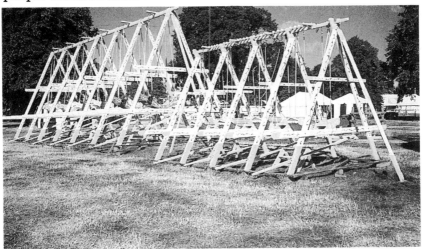

Swinging Boats.

Fighting Men

During the inter-war years and the Depression, boxing became a popular pastime and enjoyed a very large following throughout the country. For many unemployed young men, it provided not only a recreational activity, and an escape from the conditions of poverty, but also a means of making a little money, with the prospect of professional status and the 'big time'.

Some of the most depressed areas of the country provided the sport with its most famous boxers – Tommy Farr from South Wales and Len Harvey from the West Country, to name two.

Conditions for those engaged in professional boxing improved after the establishment of the British Boxing Board of Control in 1929, but prior to that time it could be a dangerous occupation with poor medical supervision and few formal regulations to protect the boxer. The fairground boxing booths drew many participants prepared to sacrifice safety for the chance to make money. Fighting could be brutal. The British Boxing Board of Control regulated entry to professional status, provided for medical attention, controlled frequency of fights and so on.

Bedfordshire Champions

'My brothers Reg, Arch and Chris, were all boxers. Arch had many knock-outs, and Reg was a welterweight, who used to travel around, boxing. Boxing was a popular sport during my youth, but many local men also boxed for money. Johnny Seamarks was one successful local boxer: Tony Arpino was another.

Boxing matches used to be held regularly at the Bedford Corn Exchange and people betted on the outcome. Also at the fair grounds, as the fairs came about once a month. Blokes from the fair would challenge someone from the crowd for money, and the match would take place in the boxing booth.

The main gym in Bedford was in the large room over the George and Dragon. There was another gym near the Rose Yard. The main one was run by Arch, and he also started the gym at the Carlton Reformatory School. Boxing used to be sponsored, and was encouraged to counter unemployment during the depression.

I've been in and out of jobs all my life. I was never able to hold a steady job for long. I've been a butcher boy, foundry worker, milkman, cab driver – all sorts. I couldn't box, as my brothers did, because of my leg injuries.'

RICHARD 'TOM' LOVELL

'My father was a boxer at one time and my brothers were always talking about boxing. Boxing was becoming a popular sporting activity then, in Bedford and elsewhere in the country. Bedford produced more boxers during the depression

of the 1920s and 1930s than any other town for miles around. Boys couldn't box professionally until the age of sixteen and by the time I was sixteen I was keen to give it a try. I got to know Boker Cox, the Bedford Modern sculler at the boathouse, who ran a gym in Tavistock Street, and he arranged a fight for me and I worked my way up from there. I practised regularly and became the Lightweight Champion of Bedfordshire.

Arthur Harvey (centre).

Among my contemporary boxers were Johnny Seamarks who was born in Oakley in 1907 and who began fighting at the age of fourteen. He had thirty-nine recorded bouts between 1925 and 1926. His total recorded bouts number one hundred and eighteen, and he became a Bedfordshire champion. Arthur Davis, my cousin, became a professional boxer in 1922 at the age of seventeen, and in over five hundred fights he was never knocked out. He won various Bedfordshire titles at lightweight and bantamweight and boxed professionally for twenty-six years. Toni Arpino, son of an Italian ice-cream vendor, went twelve rounds with the then British Heavyweight Champion, Jack London. The three Lovell brothers, Archie, Reg and Chris, numbered some five hundred fights between them. Archie's career began in 1923 and lasted sixteen years, and Chris, the youngest of the three, became welterweight champion of Bedford and retired undefeated after nine title defences. He was a contender in Paris for the European Lightweight Championship. It is said that he once declined an invitation from his nephew to train a sixteen year old by the name of Joe Bugner, later to become the British and European Heavyweight Champion! Reg Perkins, another Bedfordshire champion, and professional between 1928 and 1934, had one of this best bouts in 1933, when he fought Jack Casey, the "Sunderland Assassin", winning on points after twelve rounds. He claimed to be the only boxer in Bedford to make a living solely from boxing. Bedford was the best-paid ring in England, and he could command £4.10.0d for a twelve-round fight.

My father, George Harvey, was a keen sportsman, a boxer, cricketer and swimmer. He sparred with Jack Johnson, the World Heavyweight Champion, in an exhibition contest at the Royal County Theatre. My father's brother, Fred, trained boys at Bedford Grammar School and Toc H and two of his sons took up boxing. Fred himself was trained at the New Inn in Tavistock Street. I began training at the age of sixteen and turned professional. I took on three national lightweight champions in turn and beat them all (Packy MacFarlane, Ireland; Bobby Turnbull, Scotland; and George Reynolds, Wales). My brother and I set up our own gymnasium at one time in Brereton Road, and I remain grateful to Mr Howard, one-time Mayor of Bedford, who was a friend of my father's, and who was instrumental in helping to launch this enterprise.

During my boxing career I was managed by various promoters, one of whom was Jimmy Wilde, one-time world champion. I was fighting one night in Kilburn and Jimmy, the former Flyweight World Champion, was there at the ringside. I noticed him and he made me fight at my best. My opponent cut my eye open but I finished the fight and got the decision. Jimmy became my London Manager. Kid Burg's manager was also there, looking for a sparring partner for him. He invited me along to spar with Kid as he was preparing to fight Harry Mizler for the world title. I had three rounds in Mile End and after that he told me I was very good and asked me to return to America with him. Unfortunately I wasn't able to go. Jimmy Wilde arranged bouts for me all over London, and I sparred with many ex-boxers, including Peter McInley the Scottish champion, and Bert Buxton the Eastern Area Champion. I have fought at Euston, Hammersmith, Shepherd's Bush, Stepney, Blackfriars, which was one of the main halls, and other places. I enjoyed it because I was really fit: you can become hardened to it. I finished up doing American boxing, which is quite a different style.

You didn't get much then – about six pounds for a good fight. I was averaging six pounds per fight and had three fights in one week several times. It wasn't too tiring – it's not work you see. I've boxed in the booths, at fairgrounds and I was training there sometimes. They had rings at all the fairs then, and ran shows. This was my work, in the booth. We used to go round with a cap, collecting, and we did very well. Then I'd get a telegram telling me I was wanted at such and such a place. We were always in demand. The fairs came round much more frequently in those days, and one of the largest was Billy Woods. He would stand out in the front and draw the crowds.

I didn't suffer serious injuries. I have been put on the floor but not for the full count. I beat all the champs in turn, not for the title, but I beat them all the same, many title holders. I became Lightweight Champion of Bedfordshire. There were hundreds of boxers then, they were all out of work and trying to get money. I don't think they fight so hard now as they used to. There used to be several gyms in Bedford and there were so many good boxers doing the rounds. George Odwell of Camden Town was definitely the best boxer I ever fought and we went fifteen rounds.

I successfully applied for a Promotions Licence and became a Manager at one time. I have arranged fights at the Corn Exchange in Bedford, for various boxers, and brought the

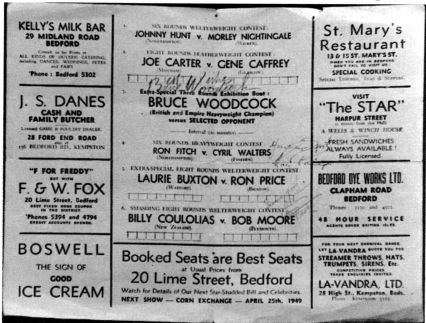

Programme of events, Bedford Corn Exchange, 1949.

Freddy Mills.

British champions of the time to Bedford. Among my distinguished visitors were Bruce Woodcock and Freddy Mills.

I've had an assortment of jobs over the years, but only took these to fit in with my boxing interests and to support myself. My wife came to England from Cyprus with her brother in 1933 and she and I met when she was evacuated to Bedford from London during the war. During our courting days she was one of my keenest supporters, and followed me around my various matches. She could shout, I tell you! I could hear her voice shouting above the roar of the crowd. I've become something of a recluse now: I detest noise and bustle and prefer my own company to that of others.

The money from boxing has been good at times, but I boxed for the sheer love of it and was an amateur turned professional. I have had more than four hundred and thirty fights and was never knocked out. There was a time when everybody in Bedford knew me or knew of me.'

ARTHUR HARVEY

The Cranfield Entertainers

'Soon after the war a group of us got together to form a concert party in order to raise money towards buying a playing field for the village. The group consisted of Mr Victor Maurice who had been a professional entertainer and was at the time manager of the Ritz Cinema, and his wife Irene, who had been a professional singer. Also in the group were Fred Lovesey, Tubby Williams, Sylvia Perrin, Ivy Picton, Edith Parker and myself. Also Vera White who played the piano.

We met in somebody's front room for rehearsals. One of Tubby's turns was mental telepathy and he tried to teach Fred how to do it. One evening we had a meeting and Fred and Tubby were practising this trick, while the rest of us sat by and watched. Fred had a bit of difficulty with the answers, but after some time I spotted how it was done and as Tubby

100

asked the questions I came out with the answers before Fred. After a while Fred turned to me and said, "You seem to be better at it than me. You had better get on with it", and so I did. After about three weeks' practice, Tubby taught me how to do it. On the night we were billed as "Tubby Williams and his Mystic". Mr Maurice dressed me up in an ornate Chinese gown and hat. He also made up my face with yellow grease paint and a drooping mandarin moustache. I sat in the middle of the stage blindfolded. Tubby then went among the audience and asked them to fetch various items out of their pockets such as a wallet, driving licence, watch, coin or banknote, comb or anything they had. Tubby would then hold up the object and ask me what it was, and I would tell them. The trick went down very well, but the audience soon saw through my disguise and remarked in loud voices, "Boo, it's only old Henry". However, nobody tumbled as to how the trick was done.

Another item was a sketch which Fred made up. The set consisted of the bare rear wall of the stage built up to represent a building site with scaffolding and a ladder and all the bits and pieces of a building site. Tubby and me were made up as a couple of gormless workmen, while Fred played the part of the foreman. After doing a few corney stunts we knocked off for dinner. I went up the ladder with a packet of fish and chips and a bottle of vinegar, and sat down on the scaffold. Tubby sat down on the floor directly underneath me and fetched out a packet of sandwiches. In the meantime I was opening the fish and chips and was sprinkling them with vinegar, most of which missed the fish and chips and went over Tubby and drenched him. As soon as he realised what was happening he picked up an umbrella and put it up over his head to keep off the rain. This caused a great deal of laughter among the audience.

After a few more crazy gags the sketch was supposed to end with one of us hoisting a bucket of cement up on the scaffold. Fred, who was in the engineering line, had made a bracket

Henry, photographed in 1976.

from steel bars with a pully wheel attached. He then had screwed the bracket to the rear wall near the top, and a rope was passed through the pully and the end tied to a bucket. When we came to do the stunt, one of us pulled on the other end of the rope to hoist the bucket. However, after a few moments the bucket stopped moving and it didn't matter how much we tugged, the bucket wouldn't budge (this wasn't in the script), so the three of us stood in the middle of the stage looking like idiots, not knowing what to do. In the end Fred climbed the ladder to see what was wrong, while Tubby and me stood by, looking on. Of course, this caused roars of laughter from the audience at the idea of the foreman doing the work, while the workmen looked on. The rope had jammed in the pully and Fred managed to free it so we hoisted the bucket and the curtain came down amid roars of laughter from the audience.

The show went very well, and we had a full house. In fact people were turned away so we decided to give a repeat performance the following week. Even then we almost filled the village hall.

We finished up by raising quite a nice bit of money for the playing field fund.'

HENRY FARRER

Entertainment in Luton

'When I was in moulding I used to go swimming after work and I'd dive in after someone else and this was how I got taught. My brother could never teach me to swim, 'though he tried. There was some fellow wounded in the war got a job with us. He came to the baths swimming, said he could swim. I dived in and he clung to me – couldn't swim – and I nearly drowned. Father knew about it before I got home. I went to have a game of billiards on the way home, and got home in the evening and he said, "I hear there was a young fellow nearly got drowned in the baths." He said I should have hit *him on the forehead, hard.*

There used to be about four Billiard Halls in Luton, one over Montague Burtons in Park Square, also one in Park Street, Leagrave Road and Gordon Street.

They used to run a Temperance Excursion to Yarmouth each year and when you walked down Regent Street it was like being in Luton. They called it Luton by the Sea. They used to take crates of beer! Cooks organised it. He had a factory, used to sell materials for the hat trade.'

FRANK CHAPMAN

Day trippers, Florence and Charlie Boyles at Great Yarmouth, 1926.

'There were small cinemas in High Town, Park Street, Gordon Street and Wellington Street, and a large one in Middle Street. Building of the Middle Street one was started by a young man and he hadn't the resources to build it. He used his parents' money and they had to give up their home. The unfinished building stood there for many years. I don't

know whether it was completed by him or handed over to another builder for completion. This was the main one. The smaller ones showed continuous films like Dr Phu Manchu – serial films. It was 4d each week, so if you saw the first part and hadn't got the money to keep going, you never knew the end! The first films with sound were not available until 1929.

There were other cinemas which closed when the big chains got a grip on the town. The small ones were closed very quickly.

Wardown Park was privately owned originally, but bought by the Luton Town Council in 1920. Up towards the Bedford end of the park there are two tombstones with the names of the children's dogs on them. I often looked at these as a child. Wardown and People's Park, which was across the Old Bedford Road, opposite Wardown, have always been popular places for walking and recreation.

Pierrots in Wardown in 1907. A variety of entertainers performed in the open-air and programmes were well supported by the Luton public. Courtesy: Luton & Neighbourhood Illustrated. Pub. T G Hobbs.

People's Park, Luton, a favourite spot with nature lovers.
Approached from the Old Bedford Road by means of a splendid
avenue of trees, this well-wooded area was visited by many
neighbouring schools – over many years – for practical lessons.
Courtesy: Luton & Neighbourhood Illustrated. Pub. T G Hobbs.

About 1935 or earlier, Luton Museum was established at Wardown. Until then the reference library at the corner of Williamson Street contained a few bits and pieces, resembling a museum. Children were not allowed in. Carnegie, who gave the library to Luton, didn't think much of the needs of children.'

CLAUDE HORWOOD

'I had a happy married life and a good social life. Tom was well-known in the bowling world and this was an activity we later came to share. I also enjoyed a game of tennis.

When ladies started playing bowls, Tom thought this should never have been allowed. He thought it dreadful. I heard that the Townwomen's Guild was forming a bowling section and I joined. Their activities should have been educational really, so eventually the bowling club broke away.

The old English game of Bowls in progress in Wardown Park, c. 1910.
Courtesy Luton & Neighbourhood Illustrated. Pub T G Hobbs.

Members of the Luton & South Beds Liberal Club photographed on
an outing to Windsor in the mid-thirties. Among these members are
many local businessmen and prominent members of the community.

The Luton & South Beds Liberal Club, erected in 1895 in Manchester Street. The property of a limited liability company, the interior was designed for the political party associated with it, whilst the shop occupying the frontage added to company revenues. Courtesy: Luton & Neighbourhood Illustrated. Pub. T G Hobbs.

We were the first bowling ladies in Luton and we started the Bowling Club which became very popular. Then the Wardown Ladies Club was formed. I went to a 40th anniversary celebration of the formation of the Bedfordshire Women's Bowling Association. Luton came into it just after that. I was Captain of the Luton Town Bowling Ladies Section, and I bowled until I was turned eighty. I've been on many tours around England, and have got quite a collection of photographs and trophies, as you can see.

I actually met my husband at the Liberal Club opposite George's Square, where they used to hold whist drives. He was in the Royal Naval Air Force during the war. He was a *staunch Liberal but he got on well in life and made things comfortable for me. He came from an old Luton family, not much background, like mine!'*

ETHEL MAYES

'I didn't get a bike until I was eleven, then my friends and I went off with a picnic lunch and stayed out all day. Tennis was one of our pleasures. There was a bandstand in Wardown Park and the theatre in the park at weekends. I was always in charge of my brother at weekends. There were punts on the lake in Wardown, and bowls. The Bowling Club always organised a Christmas party for the children of their members. My father was a member, and a member of the Conservative Club too. We went to church, and the Sunday School had an outing to Wicksteed Park for the day once a year. We had Sunday day trips with our parents in father's shooting-brake, leaving at 6 o'clock in the morning – when we could get petrol – and motoring to Clacton for the day. He put a mattress in the back so we could sleep on the way home.

The Bedfordshire Road Cycling Club on a visit to Wicksteed Park in the early 1930s. Lady members 'showing a leg', still a rare sight in those days. Photo: courtesy Mr Alec Wilmot.

We listened to the children's programmes on the radio. Sunny Stories, was a weekly magazine we looked forward to reading, and we listened to Paul Temple, Uncle Mac, and always went to bed after Dick Barton Special Agent, had finished. There was piano practice to do.

I was a girl guide based at St. Andrew's Church, Luton, in Rose Patrol, the youngest member when the patrol entered a hiking competition for the County Shield. We had to be able to read maps, arrive at a given spot at lunch-time, make a fire, cook lunch and clear up, then make our way home. The lunch that summer, 1946, was corned beef and potatoes, followed by rhubarb cooked with dried dates for sweetners. Anyway, we won the shield and there was a big jamboree which Lady Baden Powell attended, to present the shield.'

PRUDENCE HEADEY

LAW AND DISORDER

LAW AND DISORDER

Introduction

The County Police Force was founded in Bedfordshire as far back as 1840, at which time patrols were made on foot, horseback or cycle.

Prior to 1840, industrialisation was beginning to change the old rural order, even within this county, and there was emerging a certain amount of civil unrest as a result of Poor Law relief (this was a widespread phenomenon, not limited to this county). In addition to civil unrest through dissatisfaction with Poor Law dispensation, the Chartist movement for electoral and economic reform was also having its influence locally and gaining support. There were riots in Ampthill, leading to damage of the workhouse and the parish constable system of policing was beginning to be regarded as inadequate. The County Police Force was therefore established. This was Bedfordshire's first professional police force.

Conditions of employment in the police force were attractive. The police force offered financial security, and from 1890, legal entitlement to pensions on retirement after twenty-five years of service (or fifteen years if retiring on the grounds of ill-health). The availability of special housing for policemen and their families was later to become an added attraction. After 1889 the Bedfordshire Constabulary numbered ninety-one, which included seventy-seven constables who were expected to work nine hours duty in each twenty-four hour period.

From around the turn of the century matters of local concern, requiring police intervention, were as follows:

- Nuisance to ladies boating in the neighbourhood of Bedford (a matter which led to conviction for 'indecent bathing');

BEDFORD BRIDGE.

Boating on the Ouse.

- Election Day riots in Biggleswade, when labourers menaced people wearing Conservative colours;
- Bedford Pig Fraud, whereby pig breeders were advertising and receiving advance payment for livestock which was never despatched. Convictions ensued for obtaining money by false pretences;
- Disturbances and demonstrations caused by the closure of Old Priory recreation ground;
- More rigorous regulation of traffic on highways: horsedrawn vehicles, bicycles and motorcars had become the subject of government legislation (failure to use lights, drunken driving, exceeding the 12 mph speed limit). Motorcars at this time were still a rare sight in Bedfordshire;

- Rioting in Dunstable following the death of Queen Victoria (1901) and the delayed coronation festivities for Edward VII, who had fallen ill;
- A double murder in Eversholt;
- In 1905, a brickyard trade dispute at Forders works in Wootton Pillinge, after the reduction in wages;
- 1909 visit to Wrest Park by King Edward VII to spend a weekend with the American Ambassador;
- Chicken theft involving a fowl stealing ring in the Shillington area;
- Threatened widespread civil unrest at the outbreak of war, with panic buying of food, price increases and unscrupulous trading culminating in a riot in Hitchin and Dunstable;
- Murder in Leighton Buzzard in 1915;
- An attack on a naturalised British subject, German by birth, in Flitwick;
- Peace Day riots in November 1918 in Luton, when war veterans appeared to be excluded from the official celebrations and were refused the right to hold their own celebrations;
- Crash of an air balloon in 1926 at the Kempston Flower Show, where five fatalities occurred;
- General Strike of 1926 when pickets gathered at railway stations, and the Jarrow March passed through Bedfordshire, but there was no violence;
- 1929 crowd control for the launch of the R101 airship;
- 1930 crowd control as an estimated crowd of 150,000 mourned the death of the passengers and crew who perished in the R101 disaster in France;
- 1931 express train crash near the Buckinghamshire border;
- 1931 train derailment south of Leighton Buzzard;
- 1931 Whipsnade Zoo was opened, and crowd control became necessary for the large numbers of visitors;

- 1937 murder near Leighton Buzzard;
- 1939, as Britain again became engaged in war, civil defence matters assumed priority.

Memorial to those who died in the R101. The inscription reads: 'Here lie the bodies of 48 officers and men who perished in HM airship R101 at Beauvais, France, October 5, 1930'.

The Special Constable Act of 1831 made it possible for magistrates to swear in special constables in times of riot, and in 1914 new legislation rendered it possible for specials to be appointed in other circumstances. Motorised patrols of specials then began throughout the county.

The first police car to be acquired by the County Police Force was an Arrol Johnston four seater, purchased in 1913. It was not until the 1920s that the use of the motorcar for commercial and personal purposes had increased to such an extent that accidents were becoming a matter of some concern throughout Bedfordshire, with many resultant injuries and deaths. By 1928 however, the car was seen as playing a large part in the incidence of crime and to counteract this new development it was decided that the police should be in possession of motorcars and motor cycles (to be able to give chase), and that as many officers as possible should be on the telephone (county police stations were connected by telephone). It was recognised that greater numbers of police were needed for supervision and regular patrolling. The need for the police authorities to provide ambulances was also seen as important.

The Specials were obliged to use their own vehicles (motorcycles, motor cars, bicycles) for which they received mileage allowances. Wartime duties attaching to the Specials included registration and supervision of alien enemies and of Belgian refugees, billeting of troops, tracing and arrest of Army deserters, registration of pigeon fanciers and the issue of permits to breeders.

Wartime demands on the police were three-fold: civil defence work, maintenance of public order, and dealing with crime.

The special constabulary continued after the war, being, as previously, a volunteer force. The Specials were issued with blue and white armlets and truncheons. What began as an emergency measure at the outset of the war, continued as a permanent auxiliary force.

Ref. Bedfordshire Police, 1840–1990. pub. Hooley. Courtesy Andrew Richer.

The village policeman of old, is something of a romantic character, remembered as a friend to all, a figure of respect, someone who made it his business to know members of his community. The 'Bobby' was regarded as helpful, sociable and understanding: a man of principle who could inspire confidence. Mischief-making lads would be more likely to get a clip round the ear and a stern talking to than to be formally investigated, arrested and so forth. Local people trusted the village Bobby and his judgement.

The changing nature of our society has led to changes in methods of policing. No longer is one confronted with the sight of the Bobby pacing out his beat, smiling and passing the time of day with people he knows and people who have come to know him. The police presence is more likely to be recognised when a sign-written car rushes past in a flash of anonymity. Some find the sight of the police vehicle a source of intimidation. Most of us are as likely to come face to face with an alien as we are to encounter a real live policeman walking a beat. In spite of the social distance which has been created by the changing nature of policing a large community, most people would not envy the policeman his lot. Maintenance of law and order in modern Britain's cities must be a very challenging and difficult task.

Village Scandal

'When the soldiers were billeted at the big house [Haynes] there was some local scandal when one of the girls employed at the barracks, Nellie Rolt, was murdered – for jealousy it was said. Her body was found just inside Wilstead Wood, and her gravestone is in the Haynes churchyard. Only in recent years was the murderer found. He was living in Alexandra Road, Bedford, and had been a soldier. Nellie had been seeing another boy and this led to her unfortunate and untimely death. Two boys who lived in Church End, Dick Smith and Claude Lewis, found a bag belonging to her and this was how they discovered her body. They were schoolboys at the time. We all had to go to the funeral and stand at the graveside when she was buried. I believe she came from Jersey but was stationed in Haynes.

Then two other soldiers committed suicide, – one cut his throat. They are also buried in the churchyard. One of them is said to have been refused compassionate leave, and so killed himself.

There were quite a lot of women in the forces there as well as men. They had their own "pictures" up at the big house, and at one time we used to go. There was a show once a week, but you had to have someone with you to get in.

After the soldiers left, Mr Sanderson bought the place.

There have been quite a few unnatural deaths in the village over the years. Mr Allen the baker, had two sons; one shot himself and the other cut his throat. Three people were killed by lightening. The first deaths occurred during a football match, when two brothers were sheltering under a tree, down North Lane. Both were killed. On the other occasion, a man was walking across the field with a spanner in his hand and was struck down.

My husband moved to Haynes with his parents in 1919 from Biggleswade, where his father was a smallholder. He left school at twelve, during the 1914–18 war, and worked on the farm, ploughing with a team of horses – until the age of sixty-three. He was employed by Underwood and Saunders for many years, until Mr Underwood shot himself, which was only twelve months after his farmhouse was completed. Mr Saunders died some time later, from cancer.'

BEATRICE WEBB

'*Up near the George Public House [Wootton] there was a village lock-up. If the village policeman caught anyone drunk on Saturday, he would lock them up. Drunkeness was about the only crime in the village then. Boys did mischief, but we were not evil then. We created our own sport.'*

STANLEY LOVELL

'*Being a policeman, my father was once instructed to move on some Serbian gipsies who had camped where they were not welcome. He went alone at night and was received with open arms – by a large brown bear! I understood from him that his retreat was more hasty than dignified! There were numbers of Serbian or Armenian Gipsies travelling the country in covered-wagon type caravans during and after the First World War. At least we called them gipsies but they were probably refugees from war. I remember them as very dark and dressed in brightly coloured clothes.'*

GLADYS WALLIS

The Specials

'There were several "specials" in Wootton, including a grocer, farmer, coalman and baker, and they patrolled the village in pairs every night, wearing a distinctive jacket. They weren't in the police force but undertook policing duties in addition to their usual jobs. Nothing very exciting ever happened in Wootton but there were occasional drunks to be kept in order. There used to be a village keep near the church, into which deviants could be temporarily secured. If the village policeman caught anyone drunk on Saturday he would lock them up.

William Juff was a "special" and his son Bill still remembers one time when he was assigned, with a colleague, to stake-out the Chequers public house where theft of chickens had been reported. They rigged up a trip wire from a mousetrap leading to a bell in the cellar where they laid in wait. In the early hours of the morning the bell sounded and they sprang excitedly into action, only to find some unfortunate mouse had sprung the trap!

The old lock-up has gone now, so have the village stocks which we called the "pound" and which stood outside Mr Redman's – the carrier's – cottage in Bedford Road.'

FREDERICK BURRAWAY

Carlton Reformatory School

'My husband was a baker by trade and in 1941 we moved to Carlton Reformatory School for Boys, where he took the post of cook and bakery instructor. We lived in a tied house which is still standing, at this school. My husband, being a baker, had been exempted from military service.

My father had been associated with this school, where he at one time umpired the cricket matches. The school was established in the mid-nineteenth century and built by public subscription. It included a house, workshops and farm buildings. Whilst we lived at Stevington, boys were sent down

The Chequers Inn, Wootton.

from Carlton to help with the thrashing. My father made regular collections from the school whilst on his rag and bone rounds, and told us of how he had seen boys birched and salted during these visits. The Reformatory School was thought to be the last resort before Borstal – a corrective centre for wayward boys, but not like a penal institution which would leave a stain on their character.'

IVY FLUTE

'I was one of twelve children. My grandfather had been a sculler, my father was a swimmer and my brothers and sisters were all athletic. My sisters were all swimmers. My brothers Reg, Arch and Chris were all boxers. It was Arch who started the gym at the Reformatory School in Carlton, and he was there for four years. He was the first in the family to start boxing.'

TOM LOVELL

Civil Disturbances

'I was born in Luton, and lived in Biscot Road at the time of the Luton riots in 1919. They were called the Peace Day riots because 19 July 1919 had been designated a holiday for national peace celebrations. The organised events which included a banquet for Mayor Impey and certain guests, did not include any war veterans, and so the veterans decided to organise their own events including a thanksgiving service in Wardown Park, but the council wouldn't allow this.

When the day came, angry crowds gathered at the Town Hall, where the official procession greeted the mayor. There had been a great deal of anger and unrest and feelings were running high. The First World War had ended and many of the demobilised men had been upset by the attitude and actions of Mayor Impey and the Town Clerk, Bill Smith, who could be very rude and discourteous. On the afternoon of the day when the riot took place a young sailor was taken into custody by the military police, following an incident: no-one heard of him. When the soldiers marched through the town they were shouting out from the ranks – an obvious lack of discipline in regard to the forces.

The mayor fled inside the Town Hall and the angry crowds surged in and wrecked the banquet hall. Police tried in vain to guard the entrance, and some were injured in this futile attempt. There was only one mounted policeman and his horse was badly injured in the riot.

The trouble died down, but flared up again late that night, and the Town Hall again came under attack and was set alight. This riot involved a large number of people. They broke into Dickinson & Adams Garage and started the fire with petrol. A German hairdresser named Casper had his shop wrecked because he was German. Shops were looted. On the corner of Wellington Street was Farmers Music. The instruments were dragged out and played while the town hall burnt. There was a violin placed in the hole where the burnt out clock used to be.

At the time of the riot the Mayor was in the Town Hall with other people including Special Constables. They issued some people with armlets and they marched out as a file of Special Constables. The Mayor got as far as the Workhouse on the corner of Dallow Road. Within a few minutes the crowd were shouting "We want the Mayor". The Workhouse had large wooden doors and the Master got the Mayor inside and shut the doors. The master denied that the Mayor was within and fortunately the crowd dispersed.

The Fire Brigade were not able to play more than one or two hoses at once because the crowds prevented them, dragged the hydrants away, and severed them. Eventually troops were called in from an army camp at Biscot Mill, and their presence enabled the fire brigade to bring the fire under control.

After the riot, on 20 July, the Metropolitan Police were called in. It was a pointless exercise because disorderly

The Town Hall, Luton, situated at the northern end of George Street
between roads leading to Bedford and Dunstable.
Photo: Luton & Neighbourhood Illustrated. Pub. T G Hobbs.

Messrs Farmer & Company's Piano and Organ Show Rooms
in Wellington and George Street, Luton.
Photo: Luton & Neighbourhood Illustrated. Pub. T G Hobbs.

behaviour was over by then. Bill Smith said if there was another riot soldiers would be brought in and they would shoot. This was an unpopular statement. There were more disturbances and an attempt to rescue the sailor from the borough police station.

The Metropolitan Police roughed everybody up and imposed a curfew. They beat people up with batons if found at night, and locked people up.

The riot had an impression nationwide because it was the first of that type. There have been many since then. Luton was a little country market town then and the riot made national headlines.'

CLAUDE HORWOOD

The 'Common' Law

'I recall one occasion in my youth, when John Roberts, who worked for James Day at the Mansion [Harrold], was summoned for stealing from his employer, two swedes which he pleaded were for his hungry family. Despite his pleas, he was fined five shillings, about half his week's wages. The following morning the front door and steps of the Mansion were found to be strewn with the contents of several lavatory buckets. This was our local brand of "rough justice", and was not an uncommon occurrence I believe.'

ARTHUR THEW

The Police Constable

A professional, the village Bobby was dedicated to his task, playing his special part in the community, upholding the law and ensuring the safety and security of all. His special skills and commitment are deserving of a mention, and his reminiscences tell us something of community and the vicissitudes of life some years ago.

The village 'Bobby' of even fifty years ago, was a very

different representative of law and order to the police constable of today, having a much higher personal profile among local people, and because of his closer contact with the community, is generally considered to have been held in high regard. A one-man-band, pushing pedals along quiet leafy lanes, always prepared to come to the rescue when circumstances demanded a presence from the strong arm of the law. Guardian of the peace, a dedicated officer and everyone's friend – almost everyone's!

'My father was a farm worker, but when I left school my job was working as a valet at Ampthill House. One of my tasks there was exercising the horses, even though I was employed as a valet. I learned that there were vacancies in the police force and ended up joining the Dunstable Police Force in 1935, and that's where I trained. At that time Luton and Bedford had separate police forces.

I married soon after joining the police force, and realised that it really was essential for a village Bobby to have a wife, to act as unpaid assistant, receptionist and secretary. The Bobby was based in a village without radio or a car, and was really on his own. My first posting was to Ravensden, and I was responsible for

PC 71 with son John.

three villages in those early days, Renhold, Wilden and Ravensden. After the war broke out what I remember most vividly was the bombs dropping around the villages. It does seem extraordinary to think that the blitz had such an impact in a rural place, but the bombers on their way to the Midlands were jettisoning their bombs over the fields, often after they had been hit by ackack. Part of my job was to trace where the sticks of bombs had fallen in case some had not gone off. My wife was terrified, and as the bombers went over she hid with the baby in a cupboard under the stairs. I would then have to go out on my bike listening for bombs, following and working out where they were and next morning, with the Home Guard, we would go out, find the craters and walk along the line of the craters to see if they had all exploded. On one occasion a German bomber came down in my parish with the pilot still on board. He must have stayed to let the other jump out, and was dead.

The bulk of my experience of a copper's life came when I was transferred to Kensworth in about 1944. I was responsible for Kensworth, Whipsnade and Studham, and based in a police house next to the Farmer's Boy pub: the house still stands, but is now a private house. We had an enormous garden and that's when I got the bug for gardening. We stayed at Kensworth for over ten years and became thoroughly involved in local life to the extent that even now, many people in the village remember me. I got on the committee of the local Flower Show, and enjoyed village life.

There was not much crime in those days, in that locality. My job was to patrol the three villages on my bike, a lonely job down country lanes at night-time. This was point duty. Points were telephones where the police constable could be contacted. There weren't too many, but you had to be at a certain point in your parish at a given time so the sergeant, who was at Dunstable, could ring you if he wanted you urgently. That was known as 'point duty'. I had a key to the RAC box at Whipsnade crossroads so if the 'phone rang there I would be able to take the call. I also used the telephone at the transport cafe on the A5, and called there in case the sergeant wanted me.

The A5 Watling Street provided one of the main problems for me as a police constable in that area. It is a mile-and-half away from the village but goes through the parish of Kensworth and was therefore my responsibility, and there were numerous accidents. There were no road traffic patrols as we know now, and day or night, I had to be available: I was on call twenty-four hours a day. If there was an accident the phone would ring and I would either get on my bike and go down, or flag down a passing car driving through the village and commandeer a lift. I would get there and begin

John Buckledee, PC 71, directing traffic at a road accident on the A5 Watling Street, in the parish of Kensworth, just south of the Caddington turn. On the right is the entrance to Bennett House, Kensworth, once owned by Bennett's Brewery, Dunstable. The constable is wearing a peaked cap rather than a helmet: for a brief period after the war the chief constable ordered the uniform to be changed to this style.

directing the traffic. People were usually self-sufficient then, and they would do it themselves, but I would supervise. If anyone was injured (and there were no ambulances in those days), usually a passer-by would volunteer to take them to hospital. If not, it was the policeman's task to get someone to do it. If they were a stretcher case, or dead, I would call out the ambulance which was a vehicle donated by the Red Cross, and housed at the police station. One of the policemen at Dunstable would drive the ambulance out and deal with the situation. If there were dead people they would be taken to the mortuary which was in a small room behind what was then the Fire Station next to Grove House in High Street North, Dunstable, and which is still standing, and that building is just being converted into a Youth Centre.

Road accidents on the A5 were a big problem. I recall one occasion when a lorry carrying a load of fruit cake overturned. That was in the days of rationing, and it was imported to the starving British from Australia, and in the accident it became spread all over the Watling Street and was run over by all the other vehicles. It took hours to clean the road and get it off our clothes and boots. Another occasion was where a lorry carrying a load of toffees overturned. Sweet rationing was in force and villagers turned out with bags, and started collecting these toffees. I had the unpopular job of standing guard over the sweets until a lorry arrived to take them away.

The other main traffic problem was caused by Whipsnade Zoo, which was in my parish. Just after the war until the 1950s, it is hard to imagine how popular that place was. The traffic jams in Kensworth, three or four miles away, occurred every weekend. Lines of traffic going to the zoo: the road up to the common was an extension of the road from London, and it passed through Kensworth. That was the main route to get to the zoo. It became a major thing for me to have to deal with the hazards that that amount of traffic caused. On a bank holiday there could be as many as 29,000 people going to the zoo and nearly all of those people would drive through

Kensworth, coaches, double-decker buses – thirty London Transport buses in a convoy taking people out for the day. They would all have to pass the zoo gates to get to the car park and all of them would have to cross the road to get to the zoo turnstiles. It was a road-safety nightmare. I would be on duty at bank holidays and Sundays from about 10.30am until it closed after 7pm, just dealing with traffic. I used to come home worn out and on a hot day my boots were encrusted with tar. I used to get help from Dunstable but only lunch-time relief. My children looked forward to my relief arriving as the sergeant used to bring them ice-creams when he did his relief spell. That problem became so serious that subsequently the zoo donated land and money for a police house to be built nearer the zoo, so in about 1952 we moved to the new police house and I had less travelling to do. In more recent years the subway was built.

As for crime, generally speaking I didn't take too many people to court. Children in particular were more frightened of a uniformed figure than they are today. If I shouted at them it usually stopped any trouble. I used to go to the village school to give children a talk if their games were getting too wild.

I recall cycling along the lanes at dusk, near Studham, and seeing a man with a sack on his shoulder and thought he was a poacher. I approached the man and asked what was in the sack. Something started moving and it turned out it was full of live chickens. These were laying hens which the man had stolen from a farm. He dropped the sack and ran off and I gave chase. There was a struggle and he had to be arrested. If you are on your own with a bike, you can only use your handcuffs and truncheon. It had to be a serious matter before the truncheon could be drawn, and reports would then have to be made out. Serious offenders had to be handcuffed and held until help arrived from Dunstable. If a motorist passed, the vehicle would be commandeered and the offender would be driven to the cells in Dunstable. The village policeman had considerable powers of latitude in deciding whether to report someone for prosecution. If you got someone committing an offence, an entry had to be made in your pocket book so the superior officer could look at it and pursue the matter, or otherwise, as he thought fit.

Often my young son would cycle with me on my rounds, when he was about eight. We went to a farm once in Dove House Lane, Kensworth, a lonely place. The farmer had gipsies on his land and wanted them off. We cycled down to where they were and it was close to Old Hill Wood, now a very exclusive suburban estate. There was an encampment of Romany gipsies, with high-wheeled caravans and horses and they had a cooking pot with a fire and were making a stew. I cycled up and asked who was in charge, and out of the caravan came a massive figure with a black beard. My son tells me he was terrified: he'd just been reading about Black Beard! Anyway I asked when were they going to leave and Black Beard said, "Tomorrow morning we'll be off, sir", and indeed, they went and left the place spick and span, just charcoal on the ground where they had been cooking.

Later on another kind of gipsy became a huge problem, the scrap metal dealers who left a mess everywhere and would not move when you asked, until you had gone through the proper legal procedures, which was very time-consuming.

With the farming community I was responsible for enforcing the laws regarding diseases of animals. Apart from traffic duties, this was the other main thing. In those days fowl pest, foot and mouth disease, and swine fever were major concerns and I had to ensure that all sheep were dipped to stop the spread of sheep scab. This involved immersing the sheep in troughs of water treated with an arsenic-based chemical. Some of the farmers who didn't see the importance of having it done, would try to avoid doing it thoroughly and I would have to be there to see that it was done correctly. Anthrax was a very serious worry and there were cases when carcasses of animals had to be burnt under supervision. Foot and mouth prevention meant controls on the movement of animals. They had to disinfect the feet of visitors to the zoo in times of outbreaks. If a farmer was buying animals and moving them from region to region, he had to have a licence, and this caused a lot of work. I might be sleeping after being on call for twenty-four hours, and a farmer would want a licence urgently, to bring in animals, and he'd call at my home. My wife used to put paper on the floor to protect the carpets from muddy boots, until I got dressed and came down to sort it out. We had no office, and the farmer would come into the house and sit in the living room. A policeman's wife was his personal assistant, and she used to have to deal with this kind of thing. Stray dogs used to be brought to us and tied up in the yard.

The most time-consuming thing for a policeman's wife was "express messages". Scotland Yard took a more active part in regional crime then than it does now. If there was a big robbery they would circulate a description of the stolen goods so if a policeman stopped a car, he could recognise stolen goods when he saw them. The policeman's wife would receive a long list of stolen goods which she would have to write on a message pad for her husband and she would have to ring the next policeman's wife in the chain and dictate it to her so every police house would get the message. This always came on a wash day or when she was cooking the dinner, and was a very time-consuming thing for her.

There were no serious crimes locally during my time, 1945–1955. Dealing with drunks was a problem: some men, when they had had a drink, wanted to fight everybody. There was an occasion when I was injured quite seriously in an incident on the Watling Street, involving a tanker and lorry carrying fifty gallon drums of chemicals. It caught fire at the Pack Horse Café and loads of people were watching and traffic was stopping. It was a dangerous situation and I was there with the fire brigade people when the chemicals blew up. We were showered with flaming chemicals but I was wearing a big old-fashioned cape which protected me but it caught me around my neck. Some of the firemen were badly hurt and had to go to Mount Vernon Hospital. We didn't have an ambulance, and a chap with a coach company offered to drive them to hospital.

The most famous person in the village was Phillis Calvert. She had a cottage in Common Road, Kensworth, close to the Red Lion and I used to see her regularly. She frequently offered me a drink, which I politely declined, of course, but she was a very pleasant lady.

I used to spend a lot of time typing out reports on a desk in the living room of our police house. The family would be sitting listening to the radio and I would be in the corner doing my paperwork.

Later on, when I was promoted to sergeant, I was one of the first in the area to have a car rather than a motorbike. My predecessor, who used to bring the children ice-cream, had a very bad accident on a motorbike and my wife didn't want me to have one. From the '50s to the '60s there were murders and serious crimes and it got very tough. I look back fondly to the days of being a Bobby. I was initially based at Warden Hills, on the Streatley side of Luton, after promotion, and responsible for Barton, Harlington, Houghton Regis and several other villages, but the action really was at Houghton Regis, so they transferred the sergeant to there. Policemen now don't want to be living on their beat, and many of the police houses have been sold off.

The highlight of my career as a constable was going to the coronation. Each police force had to send men to London to guard the queen and they had to live in tents near the park, and turn out in the morning to be on guard duty. It poured with rain! I recall spending the whole day with so many people who had camped out and of getting friendly with them, getting the children in at the front so as to let them have a good view of the queen. Everyone was so friendly, and there was no trouble whatsoever.'

JOHN FREDERICK BUCKLEDEE

'My parents married in 1903 and my father was a police constable. He was exempted from military service, of course. He did a lot of special duty and I have spent many a sleepless night listening for him to come in. We moved around quite a lot as my father was posted in different places.

I used to hate it when my father went out on night patrol. He wore one of the old bull's eye lanterns on his leather belt. The light could be covered by a sliding shutter so as not to advertise his approach. It was a great day when he brought home his first battery torch and we were all allowed to switch it on once. We have reckoned up that his longest night patrol would have been thirteen to fourteen miles and he and all the other police were supposed to walk those distances, meeting one another at certain points at certain times.'

GLADYS WALLIS

The Magistrate

'I became a magistrate in 1957. There was no training for this but you listened for about twelve months before taking an active part. This was at Ampthill Magistrates Court. I retired after fifteen years. I attended about every two weeks during this time. Three or four times a year I attended Quarter Sessions at Bedford – that was interesting. These were cases that had been referred from Ampthill to Bedford. I was a magistrate during the time of Hanratty. The older magistrates sat and then it was referred to Quarter Sessions. There was the Juvenile Committee, Domestic Court – (divorce and custody and so on) and the ordinary court. I was on the Rural District Council, now the Mid-Beds District, and Maulden Parish Council, at the same time.'

BEATRICE WOODWARD

TRANSPORT

TRANSPORT

Introduction

During the 19th century the railways came to Bedfordshire: it is interesting to note that the London to Manchester air race of 1910 followed the course of the railway, no doubt to simplify the task of navigation in aircraft with few navigational aids. The railways expedited the movement of manufactured goods, and of vegetables and food products from Bedfordshire to the markets of London and elsewhere, and facilitated the carriage of manure and soot for fertilisation from London. It was the railways which opened up the coastal resorts during Victorian times, when Southend, Brighton and other places saw the beginnings of the tourist industry.

For ordinary folk, however, the horse-drawn vehicle was still the most popular means of travel and of moving goods, until well into the twentieth century. Horse-drawn buses operated until the First World War, and the horse-drawn fire engine and hearses were still to be seen well into the twentieth century. Despite the increasing popularity of the railways, the tram and trolly-bus, bus and private motor vehicle, the demand for horse-drawn vehicles still existed. Freight was carried in waggons, coal and liquid refreshment on drays, and farmers, market gardeners and roundsmen employed carts. Carriers plied between towns and villages carrying people and occasional goods for delivery.

One employer of large numbers of cart-horses was the railways. However, with the passing of the Transport Act of

1947, British Rail was formed from the union of four regional railway systems, and the Railway Executive then decided that all horse-drawn vehicles in the Cartage Departments were to be taken off the road. This decision led to the slaughter of working Shire horses in huge numbers.

Hansom cabs, traps, coaches were all common sights in the Victorian era, but many country folk walked or took to bicycles when these became popular and affordable. Walking for pleasure was a regular pastime, and courtship often took the form of walks in the country, by the river and over the Downs.

Bicycles were first manufactured in Bedfordshire in the late 1800s, having been designed and produced by Dan Albone, the Biggleswade inventor (1860–1906). Early bicycles took many forms, including the Penny-farthing and tandem.

It was not until after the First World War that ordinary

Maurice Boyles on his Royal Enfield, 1945. Black wheels and handlebars – no chrome for reasons of economy.

people could afford bicycles. The post in country areas was, and still is, delivered by bicycle in Bedfordshire and in other parts of the country.

Country roads were crude and often stones picked from fields would be piled up at roadsides to be used to fill potholes. Toll-gates appeared in various places on more major roads, to raise money for road repairs, but individual parishes kept minor roads in order, to a greater or lesser extent. Bridges were maintained by the County and by private subscription.

The canal system facilitated the movement of heavier freight by water – coal being one example, but also reed for thatching and a range of other goods and products. Agricultural and other cargo left Bedfordshire by this means, with Lightermen navigating the Ouse, often in gangs, assisted by boys who worked with the horses which hauled the so-called 'lighters'. Most canals nowadays are used less for commercial, and more for recreational purposes but in years gone by it was an important and viable means of transporting freight. Even until the Second World War it was used for this purpose by certain sectors of industry, and narrow boats still carry freight in some parts of the country.

Bus services began in parts of the county prior to the First World War. Passengers travelling in open-top double-deckers were provided by the bus company with waterproof sheeting which could be held over the head when it rained. During the war, Britain's buses were commandeered by the Army authorities for use as troop carriers and ambulances. The omnibus first made its appearance, and then the tram. Luton's first tram rolled out of the depot in 1905. Consisting of thirteen cars, the system was closed in 1932.

Buses have for long been the working-man's means of transport. Used for getting to work, for schoolchildren travelling to school, housewives travelling to town to shop, people going to the football match on Saturdays, cinema-goers visiting the 'flicks' or 'pictures' on a Saturday evening, or young people going to the local 'hop'. The bus was the main means of transport for people living in villages. Pull-cords, ashtrays, plush seats, blinds or curtains to screen the driver at night. The bus increased mobility and was socially important. To ride upstairs was a struggle for parents but a joy for children. The bus brought people together and people could chat whilst waiting at the bus stop and once on the bus. The bus could be heard rumbling along the road in the distance and people would run to catch it, holding their arm out at the request stop. 'Ding-dong', the conductor would ring the signal for departure and the bus would jerk, then proceed on its way. The café at the terminal would provide refreshment for drivers and passengers, who would have a cup of tea whilst awaiting departure. The destination blinds would be wound into position, passengers would board, always in the most orderly way. Once aboard the engine would roar into life, the conductor or conductress would appear, cash bag strap over one shoulder, ticket machine over the other, bell punch at waist, feet apart, hip pushed against a seat, to provide stability, the ticket punched, cash handed over, then time to chat. Over the years, drivers and passengers came to know each other and the driver would sometimes stop in an undesignated place for the passenger's convenience.

It is fair to say that the bus was the poor man's transport, as was the carrier. Many country carriers were motorising their services in the 1920s.

This century has seen the emergence of the motorised vehicle on a scale unimaginable at the turn of the century, with networks of well-maintained roads and motorways. It is hard to imagine that in 1919 Biggleswade Rural District Council was paying contractors three shillings per hour to water the dry dusty earth roads of Sandy! Eventually all roads became tarmacked.

A fleet of privately owned and operated buses photographed in the 1920s, the operator being The Reliance of Hockliffe.

Early Ventures

'The motor cycle taxi was a high-powered motor bike with a sidecar wide enough for two passengers to sit side-by-side. At that time [1920s] an ordinary motor car taxi would charge 6d(2.5p) per mile whereas the sidecar taxi would charge 4d (approximately 1.5p) per mile only.'

WALTER 'REG' PARROTT

'The first car which Vauxhall made, in about 1909, had a tiller steering mechanism. Three years before the first war they made a motor cycle with shaft drive. Only two were completed and later sold for spare parts. This was a brief venture and they did not profit from it.'

CLAUDE HORWOOD

The Carrier

'Our village carrier was Mr Hill, Keeley Lane [Wootton]. He had a type of van with two horses to draw it. There was no buses much when I was a boy, not 'til I more or less left school. Mr Hill took orders from people, brought back their groceries. It was rare for people to go, but they could go for about 2d. I remember him having this carrier's van in Keeley Lane, it was a thatched barn where he kept it. He emigrated to Canada just after the war, him, his wife and two sons went. They used to go to the Baptist Church. His daughter still lives in the same house and is about ninety-four – Mrs Copperwheat. He sold the business and his uncle, George More, bought it. He lived in Bedford Road, Mount Pleasant. He carried on the business until the advent of the buses.

The bus first run from Wootton was run by the Ansteys from Cranfield. It had solid tyres and the speed limit was seven miles per hour. He had a cousin in Bedford called Staffen, who drove a Foden steam waggon for Grey, Caudwell Street. He was summonsed for driving one at seven miles an hour!'

STANLEY LOVELL

'The carrier's cart used to operate between Wootton and Bedford before the buses came along. This held about eight people and the charge to Bedford was 4d. Dicky Lowe was the operator, and there was another operated by Mr Hill at Keeley Lane [Wootton]. His daughter Mrs Copperwheat, still lives there, and is now in her nineties.'

FREDERICK BURRAWAY

The Tram

'It was in 1905 that the first tram left the Luton depot, and they continued to run throughout the period of the Great War. There were four routes: one to London Road, one to Chapel Street, one to Dunstable Road and then High Town and Round Green. They were very visible but there was one serious

A Luton tram in George Street. One of the last-surviving open-topped double-decker trams has recently been bought by the Council and is to be re-built. The Friends of Luton Museums are contributing to the cost.

Wooden, reversible bench seats in an early tram.

accident. One tram missed the turning at the bottom of Midland Road. It should have turned left and gone into Middle Street but it went on and hit a hoarding at the bottom of Midland Road.'

CLAUDE HORWOOD

'The modern cars all had eight wheels which made a rapid donk, donk – donk, donk sound on the rails. Stopping and starting was accompanied with the loud hiss of air brakes now common on trucks and buses but in those days restricted to the trams. There was also a distinctive but pleasant smell associated with sparking in the motors. These cars were more comfortable and faster than the contemporary buses.

The older cars were more typical of other systems: these had only four wheels and pitched rather badly at higher speeds. Seats in the lower saloon were usually long benches along the sides, more often than not wooden and without upholstery. Standing passengers, on which there was normally no limit, held on to leather straps hanging from the ceiling, and stood on the feet of the seated persons whose feet were of course in the standing area. This was not often a problem for me: being in the charge of maiden aunts I had to give up my seat to adults, having first raised my school cap if said adult was female! This could these days be a reason for abhorrent behaviour in later life! My preference anyway was to stand at the door at the end of the saloon and watch the motorman, as the driver was called. He (or in some few cases she) stood at the controls of the older cars turning a handle with his left hand to control the speed and his right hand the large brass handle on the brake. On newer cars the driver perched his bottom on a small seat in the fashion of a shooting stick. In this case the brakes were air-operated from a small lever in the driver's right hand.

Some of the really old cars had no windscreens or protection for the driver, who except in the very warmest weather, wore a heavy coat and big leather gloves. In wet weather he wore a large waterproof cape.

The guard, as the conductor was usually called, carried a wooden rack of tickets which he pulled off one at a time and punched a hole in it to show the limit of your travel. When he punched the ticket the machine rang a bell hence the name "Bell Punch". If the bell didn't ring it meant he had not punched the ticket and had to have another go. The tickets were different colours for different prices and the small round piece punched out was retained in the punch and these could be counted later to check the guard's takings were correct. On old cars the guard rang the bell for the motorman by pulling on a leather strap that ran under the ceiling of the saloon. This also produced a slapping sound as it hit the ceiling.

When not in the charge of the aforementioned aunts my brother and I would always go upstairs. Regulations meant that trams were about nine inches narrower than today's buses so the seats and aisles were consequently narrower. The people however, were not narrower and when the top deck was full they overlapped the seats, virtually blocking the gangway. On the older cars the stairs to the top deck were normally in a tight spiral and steeper than bus stairs. They had several brass handrails to help one climb.

Trams seldom turned around at the end of a journey, they were mostly double-ended and at a terminus the driver took the key from the controller and his shooting stick stool if he had one, from one end to the other. The guard walked along turning the seat backs over to face the other way. Then he took hold of the rope which was attached to the trolley which collected the electricity from the overhead wire and pulled the trolley from the wire. He then walked around the car pulling the trolley and then allowed it to spring up behind the car onto the wire again. This was not always accomplished first time. If it was dark of course, the lights went off when the trolley left the wire and they flashed on and off each time the trolley touched the wire until it was finally in place. The tram then went off in the opposite direction.

Tram-lines were normally in the middle of the road so at

stops passengers had to walk out into the road to get on. This was not too much of a problem because there was not much other traffic about. Tram services were quite frequent in big towns in peak hours. Trams would run at one-minute intervals. This meant that there was always a tram in sight. If there was a queue at a tramstop it moved out from the pavement to the side of the car and when one car left full, the queue stayed in the road for the next tram – and so on – and the road traffic either stopped or went around the tram queue!' ANON

The Bus

'Fountains Road [Luton] was the end of the terminal: the bus stood at the end of the road. The route took it through the town and up to Cutenhoe Road, and it was a journey we children would do at the weekend, to go to Stockwood Park. The bus had wooden slat seats and there was a big clock at the end of the road, which stood on four legs, for the bus driver's reference I suppose. Nobody had a private car, and we had to rely on the buses.

Because my grandparents lived in Stevenage, I was occasionally put on the bus from Hitchin to Park Square. I can remember coming back one morning: grandfather had a petrol allowance and he put me on the bus Monday morning, the workers' special, to Vauxhall. I can still smell the men in their oily overalls. We came up Offley Hill so slowly that the policeman who was walking up the hill, lifted his bike on the bus to ride to the top of the hill!' PRUDENCE HEADEY

'The bus service started gradually in Luton and the first regular service was between Luton and Hitchin. The routes were not clearly defined and on one occasion, when I was a passenger, the driver and conductor could be heard discussing the route they should take! By 1925 a regular bus service with established routes to various local places, was in operation.' CLAUDE HORWOOD

'Years ago you were isolated from the passengers and stuck in an uncomfortable cab most of the time. It was not until you got to the turn around point that you got in the back with the conductor for a chat and a cigarette. The cab was poorly heated and sometimes there was no heating at all. No power steering and often crash gear boxes in those days. It was not a very enviable job. Buses were rather under-powered and they would grind their way up hills, often with a full load and standing passengers.

On Saturday, being the busiest day of the week, the conductor would be up and downstairs hundreds of times a day and it cannot have been an easy job. On Saturday the buses were often full up with standing passengers and the scene could be very jolly and affable if the conductor was a bit of a comedian. There was a lot of friendly banter going on.

Upstairs would be full of smoke, often with no windows open. There was a fog of cigarette smoke, as most men would smoke on their way to work and in wet weather the glass would be streaming with condensation. The conductor would be quick, with his leather satchel and ticket machine (or a wad of tickets marked with various prices and all he did was punch a hole in the appropriate ticket). "Conductor or conductress" I should say, as many women worked on the buses. Quite a few of the drivers would have their wives as conductresses and it was the conductor or conductress that made the journey an enjoyable experience, or otherwise. Some of the conductors had a way with women. They all had their distinct characteristics.

Apart from Saturday, the busy times were between 7.30 and 9.00, taking office workers and school children to their destinations. The women would jump on in the morning, smiling, smelling of perfume and looking fresh and smart. It was a different picture at the end of the day on the return journey home.

In the summer it was quite pleasant, but when one-man buses started the driver was put under some pressure. That *would have been about twenty years ago. Some of the older drivers would not take on those one-man operations because the additional wages did not warrant the extra work and responsibility, having to cash-up at the end of the day and taking responsibility for the work of two people. The younger ones took to it much better than the older ones entrenched in their ways. Younger drivers enjoyed the opportunity to chatter with the passengers, especially the ladies.*

Inspectors would be quite a common sight, lurking behind trees and boarding the bus unexpectedly to check on running times, punctuality of the bus and to check the tickets!

Late Saturday nights were rather raucous. People would get on the bus after a night at the pub and would often start an argument. Drunks often didn't want to pay their fares and would start arguing over silly little things.

Relief buses were quite common on Saturdays in my childhood but it was not uncommon to be left standing at the bus-stop with your hand out. Some drivers would nonchalantly drive past, looking the other way.

If the conductor was on the top and not near the bell-push he would stamp on the floor or kick the bulkhead to signal departure. On more than one occasion I can remember the conductor getting off to go to the public convenience and children pushing the bell. Off would go the bus, leaving the conductor behind!'

ANON

The Trains

'For many years, as late as 1930, the majority of trains from Bedford to St. Pancras did not stop at Luton. There was a guard who was not fully conversant with the right moment to release a slip coach at Luton for passengers disembarking, and it sometimes went past the Luton Station or did not reach it. Sometimes people had to get down on the line because the carriage had careered past! A horse was used to pull it back occasionally. On one occasion the guard so badly judged the

moment for release that it went through to the next station before it stopped. The slip coach was the last coach on the train and was coupled in a different manner so the guard released the coupling and the coach carried on under its own momentum until it stopped. It probably could not be stopped independently. The date these were last used may have been about 1930. Bedford was a larger and more important place than Luton at that time.

The Ludlow and Wernher families gave a service to the town. The station on the Northern Line, "Luton Hoo", would not have existed but for the influence of these families. Lady Ludlow's husband died and left her five million pounds around 1920. She then re-married a wealthy man.'

CLAUDE HORWOOD

The Cycle

'I met my husband-to-be going up Tollgate Hill towards Sharnbrook. I couldn't afford the buses so I walked everywhere. He passed on a bicycle and asked me the way. He was from Stagsden, where his father kept the White Horse Inn. We then met for a first date at Radwell Bridge and my mother came along as chaperon. She approved of him, took his bike and allowed us to go walking. My boyfriend and I later bought a tandem to save twelve shillings a week on bus fares, while we saved to get married. I still have a snapshot of this tandem.'

IVY FLUTE

'From 1930 my leisure was mostly cycling. In 1931 I joined the Bedfordshire Road Cycling Club and I am a life member, although I no longer ride with the Club. Last Sunday I did a short sponsored ride for charity – twenty+ miles – in the sweltering heat. I must have been forty years or more older than most of the others taking part! We got to one point where the organisers had drawn a line across the road at the foot of a hill. We were all told to dismount and they timed us individually as we rode up this hill! Mine wasn't the fastest time, but not quite the slowest either. It was all part of the "Commitment to Get Fit" programme for muscular dystrophy.

Originally the Bedfordshire Road Cycling Club used the Scouts Hut in Cardington Road, and it was not until after the war that we built our own Club House. There were both male and female members. I had a Claude Butler bike which was built about 1934, and that was built to my own size and specification. I think it cost about £20, but at that time you could buy a bike for £3, so it was quite a lot of money. There were few gears then, most Club riders used fixed wheel. Claude Butler still make cycles, I believe, mountain bikes and that sort of thing.

I've cycled over much of the country and on the Continent. In fact I kept a log from July 1931 until my tour of Germany in 1937. That was a detailed photographic log, with recorded mileages, which is still in my possession.'

ALEC WILMOT

Alec's log begins with an excursion to Hunstanton, 6–12 July 1931, and reads:

'We (that is Stan and I) left Cardington at 4.35am on the 6th July for Hunstanton; the grey of dawn was just tinting the sky as we wheeled our cycles, complete with camping kit, etc. on to the road and set off toward the village of Cople, the first place en route for Eaton Socon, and Huntingdon. The road for the most part, to Huntingdon, is not of very great interest, being the main road to the north. At Huntingdon we turned right for St. Ives, along a road of just a little more interest, and here the world around seemed to be waking itself up a bit from its sleep: here we saw a milkman, and there a cowman or horsekeeper going early to his work, while all around was more distinct, as the sun began to reveal the fields and hedges . . .'

The Motor Car

'I did my first driving in Mr Juffs' car at the bakery, when I was about sixteen or seventeen. He used to let me drive it around the yard. A Citroën it was, just a family car. There were no lessons as such, or tests, in those days.'

FREDERICK BURRAWAY

'Until the mid-1890s the use of motor cars in the United Kingdom was positively discouraged; in fact there was little, if any, incentive to own one, and at least one English owner kept his car in France for use on French roads only. This arose because drivers in Britain were operating under the Locomotive on Highways Amendment Act of 1878. This set a speed limit of 4mph in the country and 2mph in towns and demanded that vehicles must be preceded by a man on foot, though the rule, dating from 1861, that he had to carry a red flag was rescinded. These rules were aimed at the operators of heavy steam traction engines used in agriculture and for pulling heavy loads, for steam ruled on the roads as well as the railways, and the railway lobby saw to it that the successful steam coaches and omnibuses which had operated between 1820 and 1835 carrying fare-paying passengers had to pay such high tolls that by 1855 they had been legislated out of existence.

Private cars only became viable in the United Kingdom from November 14th, 1896, known as "Emancipation Day", when the Light (Road) Locomotive Act became law, doing away with the necessity for a man to walk in front of every vehicle and raising the speed limit to 12mph. To celebrate this a famous run from London to Brighton was organised on the day the Act became law in which thirty-five vehicles set out from London and twenty-two arrived in Brighton after various vicissitudes, powered by petrol, steam or electricity (although the latter could only manage some twenty miles before the batteries ran down and Brighton was all of fifty miles from London).

1904 2-seater Vauxhall 6hp single-cylinder. Fuel consumption approx. 37mpg. Top speed 18mph. Price when new about £150. A London to Brighton competitor since 1950. Photo: courtesy Vauxhall Motors Ltd.

All the vehicles were of foreign manufacture and some were foreign entries, either French or German, with one car, a Duryea, coming all the way from the USA. The Duryea, driven by Frank Duryea, and two noisy French Bollée 3-wheelers driven by Leon and Camille Bollée, were the first to arrive at Brighton, witnessed by immense crowds all along the route in the appalling wet weather which featured throughout the day, and which has often been repeated in the annual November drive to Brighton by pre-1905 cars, held since 1927 to commemorate the original run.

Although a German, Karl Benz, had been the first man to sell cars to the public from 1890, after producing his first car, a rear-engined 3-wheeler, in 1885, and his countryman, Gottleib Daimler, had produced the first motor cycle in 1885 and the first 4-wheeled car in 1886, it was the French who had originally developed car design in the 1890s through holding many contests for them from the Paris–Rouen Trial of 1894 to the Paris–Bordeaux–Paris and Paris–Marseilles–Paris races of 1896 and the Paris–Amsterdam–Paris race of 1898 and many others. Winning speeds went up from 11mph of the Paris–Rouen to 40mph in the Paris–Toulouse–Paris race of 1900. The French firm of Panhard Levassor had pioneered and popularised their cars, initially with Daimler engines, using engines at the front from 1891 with rear wheel drive and were thus setting the trend followed by most of the future cars of the 20th century.

In the early days, punctured tyres were the motorists' most common problem after steel-shod wheels and those with solid rubber tyres had been abandoned for the obvious advantages of pneumatic tyres. The situation was not helped by the fact that road wheels were not detachable, so fitting replacement tyres and tubes was awkward, and it was not possible, of course, to carry and fit a spare wheel. The first big improvement was the detachable rim, from 1906, which could be changed almost (but not quite) as easily as a spare wheel once detachable wheels became the norm. Other problems were the distinct lack of garages from which to buy petrol, so that chemist's shops had to be visited to buy benzine or, alternatively, "oil shops". For repairs, there was always the hope that cycle shops could help, especially those who also catered for motor cyclists, whilst blacksmiths could help with some repairs.

In April/May, 1900, the Automobile Club of Great Britain & Ireland, which became the Royal Automobile Club in 1907, held the 1,000 Mile Vehicle Trial from London to Edinburgh and back, observing the 12mph speed limit in England and 10mph in Scotland. British cars amongst the best twelve of the sixty-five starters and thirty-five finishers included Napier, Wolseley (designed by Herbert Austin) and British built Daimlers.

1903 was the next big landmark in British motoring history when the New Motor Car Act raised the speed limit to 20mph as from January 1st, 1904, and the most remarkable thing about that is it remained the law until the 1930 Road Traffic Act abolished the speed limit altogether from January 1st,

1931. Fortunately a banked racing track had been built in 1907 at Brooklands, near Weybridge in Surrey, where manufacturers could legally test their cars at speeds up to over 130mph in the interim.

The Road Traffic Act, 1934, reimposed a speed limit in built-up areas only of 30mph, whilst from December 22nd, 1965, an overall speed limit outside built-up areas of 70mph was introduced. Today the limit is 60mph on ordinary roads but 70mph on twin track roads and motorways.

In 1904 Louis Rigolly in a French Gobron-Brillié car put the Land Speed Record up to 103.56mph at Ostend, and it is noteworthy that the Silver Ghost Rolls-Royce, which made its first appearance in 1906, was good enough to continue to be made, with very little change, until 1926. Petrol deliveries were made in cans until 1920 when the first hand operated pumps were installed, drawing fuel from underground tanks. Most pumps were still hand operated throughout the 1930s. The first traffic lights were installed in Piccadilly, London, in 1926.

It is recorded that an early car owner, the Duke of Bedford, had become so used to stopping to change to fresh horses to draw his carriage on his way to London that when he became a car owner he used to have a second car sent on ahead so that he could stop at the same place and get into a fresh car!

More important so far as Bedfordshire was concerned, in early 1905 the makers of Vauxhall cars since 1903 moved from Vauxhall in London to a new site on the outskirts of Luton where they built high quality luxury, sporting and racing cars until in 1925 they were taken over by General Motors of the USA, after which less expensive mass-produced family saloon cars were made on which advanced features in the 1930s like synchromesh gearboxes (1932), independent front suspension (1935) and, in 1937, unit construction (no separate chassis) were introduced. Just after the war it was possible to buy a Vauxhall with a heater and radio, as optional equipment only, thus giving the car all the comforts of the home, even in "Emancipation Day" weather.'

PETER HULL

FIRE FIGHTERS

Church Street Fire Station built in 1901. Described as having been fitted with modern appliances necessary to cope with any outbreak. The Head Constable was in 'telephonic communication with all firemen'. An efficient brigade in its day.
Photo: Luton & Neighbourhood Illustrated. Pub. T G Hobbs.

FIRE FIGHTERS

Introduction

Today's modern, high-speed fire-fighting tender is a far cry from fire-fighting equipment of yesteryear. Even after the turn of the century, fire-fighting was a service run by volunteers. Fund-raising made possible the provision of waterproof uniforms, and fire tenders were horse-drawn, with pumps so that water could be drawn from streams or standpipes. An early development which marked progress, was the tender which contained its own water tank. In the latter years of the nineteenth century, payments of sixpence were being made to volunteers for attendance at drill nights, with an additional sixpence for greasing the leather hosepipes and cleaning the engine gear! When fire broke out, runners were sent to locate the volunteer firemen and the horses then had to be rounded up and tacked up to the tender. Later, sirens were located at the fire station, so the alarm could be sounded to alert the fire brigade. From the days of the messenger, developments have included the siren, telephone and pocket alerter. The modern fire-fighting force is well paid and well trained for the job.

Fire and Firemen

'The fire engine was housed in a building in the centre of the village [Sharnbrook] and the master baker named Newell, was the chief fire officer. If a fire broke out he would raise the alarm to the other firemen and with his two horses or those of the local carrier, the fire engine would be drawn to the scene

of the fire. Returning home from work one evening someone told us that a fire had broken out in the small village of Radwell. My father and I hastened to the scene to find the thatched roof well ablaze; one of the firemen shouted "All hands to the pump". This was a manual pump operated by alternating wooden bars on either side. It needed at least four men on each side, to press down the wooden bar. Water was obtained from a pond in the adjoining field, as there was no other available nearer than the river, pumped water being unheard of in those days. The water buckets used were made of stout leather.

This fire engine now stands in Bedford Museum.'

WALTER 'REG' PARROTT

'It will be of historic interest to note that both Blunham and Sandy had fire-engines prior to 1860. In 1862 the "Vestry" (Parish Council) of Blunham invited Moggerhanger to subscribe £10 towards the cost of building a "Fire engine house". The men who manned these engines were all volunteers and, from a photograph in the Fire Station at Sandy, it is seen that these men assumed the rather exotic titles of Captain, Lieutenant, Engineer and Brigadier which now have the equivalent of Fire Officer, Leading Fireman and Fireman.

One amusing item about the Sandy Fire Brigade is that "in March of 1880 it was decided that, if any man had to be replaced for any reason, his replacement must be of the same physical proportions so that he could wear the uniform of the man who he replaced".

To call out the Fire Brigade one had to continue to ring a large bell hung outside the Station; "Call boys" who lived nearby would then mount their cycles and go round the town alerting the Firemen.

The first "Engines" were horse-drawn but were later followed by "Steamers" and, in 1900, Sandy took possession of a magnificent "Double Vertical Steam Fire Engine" that cost

The Biggleswade Fire Brigade.

the Urban District Council £329. This engine could throw 260 to 300 gallons of water to a height of 150 feet through a one-inch vent. On its arrival it was "Christened" at a civic reception after which it was paraded through the streets led by three brass bands and a large procession.'

H S BROWN

'If wet when stacked, a haystack could combust and catch on fire. There was a fire engine in Woburn, horse-drawn, but if fire broke out they had to catch the horses first. It was a familiar sight in August time, when many stacks caught fire. They might use a manual pump or steam, and draw water from a well, or pond. Fire fighting was voluntary in Woburn originally.'

CHRISTOPHER CREAMER

'During the First World War there was a munition factory at Chaul End. There was a fire or an explosion during this time, but it was kept secret and no-one knew the details of it. Shortly after the end of the First World War there was a fire

at Laporte's factory in Kingsway. All the contents were shooting up through the roof, chemicals exploding. The fire brigade did not have the means of dealing with chemical fires. It was gutted.'

CLAUDE HORWOOD

'In 1921 we had the best summer I can remember. A real drought. I was twelve. It was customary for all the people in the village to fetch water for washing from a clay pit in Fields Road, with clean dustbins, barrels, etc. Water was so scarce, you had to rely on wells and pumps. At the bottom of Cause End Road where I lived we were fortunate in having a pump that all the summer never ran dry. Mr Keep the baker at Hall End – his wife was Mr Lunnis's sister, – he fetched water from Hall End to make his bread because they were so short of water at Hall End. Farmers were having to fetch river water for their cattle. A big problem in drought conditions is fire, of course.

When I was a lad of around fifteen, there was a thatched public house on fire at Cranfield and the nearest Fire Brigade was Bedford. The tender went through the village drawn by four black horses one Sunday lunchtime. This image, of the horses galloping through, still stands out very vividly in my memory. It was a fascinating sight to see the speed they were going. They were fine horses and they could run. The Bedford Fire Service was in Mill Street, Bedford. The fire station was erected in 1889 to accommodate the Merryweather Steam Fire Engine, presented to the Borough by the ninth Duke of Bedford. The fire station contained apartments for the resident firemen. It was customary for the steam engine to be lighted as soon as the alarm sounded, and the brass-helmeted firemen seated themselves in rows, one on each side of the engine. At the scene of the fire the nozzles of the hoses were often placed in the river, and the pump started. It wasn't until the mid-1930s that water was actually piped to the villages.'

STANLEY LOVELL

'I belonged to Shefford Fire Brigade for thirty-two years. We used to go to Cambridge overnight and other places, came home and worked in the day at the mill. During the war this was. Every fifth night we were on all night. Next night off and the next night we went if the siren went. I was an Officer-in-Charge. Fire always seemed to start in the night and during the blackout light couldn't be seen. I was in the London region during part of the Second World War.

We went to the Turners fire in Bedford between the Arcade and Lime

Frank Perridge, Shefford Fire Brigade.

Street. Turners had a big furniture warehouse, it ran right along to Lime Street.

They had a steam fire engine in Mill Street, Bedford: burnt coal. I was asked to drive it. It blew off steam but there was a safety valve. I knew what to do because I had worked for so long with the steam engine in the yard. A pair of horses used to pull it. By the time you got to the fire you had steam to pump the water up. The Shefford Fire Station is now the Council Chambers.

Years ago we held a jumble sale to buy the coal, and one to buy the uniforms! It was all voluntary. The Council took it over just before the Second World War.

I have a medal for thirty years' service, inscribed "Exemplory Fire Service", which I received in 1955.'

WILLIAM 'FRANK' PERRIDGE

'In 1914 when my father was fourteen years old there was a volunteer fire brigade in Stevenage, and he was one of their members. The first thing he had to do when they had a call was to go to the meadows to catch the horses to harness them to the fire tender. That was his job, to catch the horses. The water was hand-pumped out of the tanker. He used to say they delighted in pulling houses to pieces to make sure there was no fire still smouldering in the thatch.'

PRUDENCE HEADEY

HIGH FLIERS

The Wright brothers. Photo: courtesy The Shuttleworth Collection

Aerial warfare, First World War.
Photo: courtesy The Shuttleworth Collection.

HIGH FLIERS

Introduction

The early years of this century saw the beginnings of flight, and the trials and tribulations of the flying machine. Only those with vision, initiative and considerable financial resources could involve themselves in this exciting new development. As nations competed for gain in the field of aviation, the country saw the emergence of the brave aviator and his flying machine – regarded in the early years as rather more an instrument of pleasure and source of amazement, than as a serious mode of transportation. The flying circuses emerged, and the concept of aerobatic stunt flying and pleasure flights.

The first man-carrying aeroplane flight by Orville Wright took place in December 1903, when his aircraft covered about a hundred and twenty feet in twelve seconds. By 1905 brothers Wilbur and Orville were able to fly a distance of twenty-four miles. In July 1909 the Frenchman Louis Bleriot flew across the English Channel. 1927 saw the first solo trans-Atlantic flight by Charles Lindbergh.

In Britain millionaire businessmen vied for publicity in promoting flight, offering large rewards for distance flights. Of those with the means, there was no shortage of candidates willing to compete. These events drew large audiences and much publicity.

At the outset of the First World War aeroplanes were used for reconnaissance purposes. Some time into the war, their potential use as instruments of war was recognised and men commenced to shoot at each other, using hand-guns, seated in open-cockpit (and linen-covered) aircraft! This was taken a step further with the use of guns mounted on the fuselage of the aircraft. In 1915 one innovative French flying ace reinforced his propeller with steel so that the gun, mounted on the fuselage, could be aimed forwards and fired without damaging the propeller. However, this idea proved fatal in the end, when he shot off his propeller whilst engaged in action with the enemy, and crashed to his death. This led to the development (by a Dutch designer) of synchronised prop. rotation and simultaneous gunfire. This was truly the birth of the fighter 'plane. Many subsequent innovations occurred, brought about by the fighter aces themselves rather than through Government or Military leadership.

The first pilots conscripted had all financed their own flying tuition: many had logged very few hours and were inexperienced pilots, untrained in the nature of aerial warfare and tactics, since aeroplanes were not at that stage regarded as instruments of attack. However, only two weeks after the war began a German pilot leaned out of his aircraft and dropped, by hand, bombs over Paris. The use of pistols led on to the dropping of bombs, and machine gun fire. Aerial warfare gained momentum. The most notorious of the enemy aces was a brilliant tactician, a feared yet respected Prussian aristocrat by the name of Manfred Von Richthofen, known as the Red Baron. Aerial warfare consisted of dog fights involving up to a hundred aircraft, all manoeuvring for advantage, an activity described as 'a mad man's night out'. The Red Baron came to be a master of the art. Six hundred and forty-four allied planes were shot down during the course of the war. However, the war itself gave impetus to and promoted developments in aircraft design and aeronautical engineering. These were times of great innovation and the aces of war were the masters of the evolving technology. The Royal Flying Corps formed in 1912, together with the Royal Naval Air Service, (formed in 1914), came to be known, in 1918, as the Royal Air Force.

Whilst enthusiasm and interest in aircraft grew, another pioneering development was taking place: that of the airship. The Royal Airship Works and the Airship Programme of 1924–30 saw the design, development and production of the enormous airships R.100 and R.101, the pride of Cardington, and indeed, of a nation intent on perfecting flight and aiding world communications and travel. Tragically, the R.101 was lost on her inaugural flight to India, when she crashed in Beauvais, France, on 5 October 1930. Sad as this event was, the people of Cardington, Bedfordshire were at the forefront of aeronautic development during the inter-war period, and instrumental in promoting flight. Although the programme was abandoned, the initiatives and endeavours which led to the phenomenon of the airship and projected long-distance travel, undoubtedly played their part in the subsequent development of aircraft capable of long-haul flights.

Many of Bedfordshire's communities have been connected with flight over the years: Henlow, Thurleigh, Tempsford, Cranfield, Little Staughton, Chicksands (USAF base) and Leighton Buzzard, war-time headquarters of the RAF Signals organisation. The most well-known centres of aviation are probably Luton, Cardington and Cranfield, but of world renown is the unique Shuttleworth Collection in Old Warden, a Trust established in memory of the founder of the collection, Richard Shuttleworth, a regular place of pilgrimage for aircraft enthusiasts the world over.

Inspiration

'When I was ten, my brother Jimmy, a friend of Richard Shuttleworth, borrowed Richard's DH Moth and gave me my first flight, which created a lasting impression on me and aroused in me a keen desire to become a pilot. This aeroplane, G-EBWD, is still in the Shuttleworth Collection, and I still fly it. I must be the only person to be still flying the same aircraft after fifty-seven or fifty-eight years. My last flight in G-EBWD was in the summer of 1989, when I flew to Ipswich to a rally.'

WING COMMANDER OLIVER WELLS

The DH60X Moth which was crash-landed by Richard Shuttleworth and Jimmy Edmunds in France. Still flown by Oliver Wells.

Airships

'I got a job at Cardington where I had to press out the skins to make the outside of the airships. I was working there when the R101 went down. The skins were taken out of a pail and spread on a frame. The Skin Department Forelady, Maud Keens, was also from Haynes. I remained there until we were made redundant after the R101 disaster. It was on 4 October 1930 that the R101 took off from Cardington to fly to India. Weather conditions deteriorated and she crashed in Beauvais, France. This was her maiden voyage. Fifty-four passengers and crew perished. In the Cardington cemetery, opposite the church, is a mass grave in which the dead were interred. Only six people survived the crash. The R100, which was still under construction, was scrapped.'

BEATRICE 'MAY' WEBB

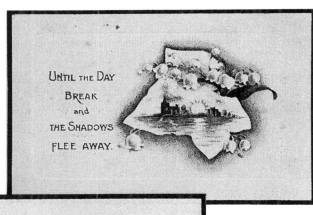

UNTIL THE DAY

BREAK

and

THE SHADOWS

FLEE AWAY.

In Ever Loving Memory

OF

Lord Thomson, Air Minister
Sir Sefton Brancker
Lt.Col. V C Richmond
Lt-Commdr N G Atherstone
Major P Bishop
Major G H Scott
Chief Coxswain Lotter
Wireless Operator Elliott
G Watkins
R B Colmore
Ft.Lt H C Irwin
Sq-Ldr E L Johnston
Mr. C A Giblett
Sq-Ldr F M Rope
Fly.-Officer E H Steff
Ft-Lt William Palstra
G K Atkins 30
R Blake 30

J Hodnett 29   Steward
G W Hunt 41   Chief Coxswain
S T Keeley 35
T A A Key 35
W H King 20
M F Littlekit 29
S H Mason 33
J W Megginson 18 Galley Boy
W Monie 30
A W J Norcott 29
A Bushfield
Sq-Ldr W H L O'Neil
L F Oughton
W G Radcliffe 31
M G Rampton 31
A J Richardson 29
E G Rudd 25
P A Foster

C J Fergusson 36
H E Ford 27
W R Gent 53   First Engineer
E A Graham 28   Cook
C A Burton
A C Hastings 30

A H Savidge 32
S E Scott 40
G W Short 34
C E Taylor 33
J Buck Lord Thomson's attendant
Samuel Church

WHO LOST THEIR LIVES IN THE AIRSHIP R 101 IN FRANCE

Sunday 5th October 1930

IN THE MIDST OF LIFE WE ARE IN DEATH

By kind permission of H.M. the King, the lying in State
will be in Westminster Hall

A loss so great, a shock severe
To part with those we loved so dear,
Though great the loss, we'll not complain
But trust in Christ to meet again.

Printed by S. Burgess, 8 York Place Strand, W.C.2

Card of remembrance for those lost in the R101.

The Shuttleworth Collection

'My good friend Richard Shuttleworth learned to fly at Moorpark Aerodrome, Renfrew, from about 1931, and at Brooklands, where he was taught by George Lowdell. He bought his first aeroplane in 1931. My first flight with Richard was to Chelmsford and this fired my enthusiasm for flying.

Not very long after our flight to Chelmsford, on May 7, 1931, when Mrs Shuttleworth had gone over to the continent for a health check-up, Richard and I set off from Old Warden in a DH Moth – G-EBWD – to fly there. Mrs Shuttleworth had given Richard a flask filled with brandy and the first night we spent near Calais, where there was an airfield. The man who ran the place was an Englishman who had remained there with his girlfriend instead of returning after the 1914–18 war. Palmer was his name. It was cold and the flask we passed from one to the other whilst sitting on a bed which we had to share, and watching the carpets being blown up from the floor. The next day we set off for Clermont Ferrand but the cloud came down to ground level as we flew over the Massif Central in pouring rain, and we got lost. Richard decided to land, so we came down over some trees and landed heavily in a field, forcing the undercarriage up through the wings. Fortunately neither of us were injured, and the farmer arrived with a large farm waggon which we used to transport the dismantled aircraft to one of his barns. We then arranged for a truck to be sent to transport the unfortunate aircraft to Gannard Station where we loaded it into a wagon and consigned it to Morane Saulnier's works at Villacoublay on the outskirts of Paris. Mrs Shuttleworth was instrumental in providing transport to ferry the parts of the aircraft around. From Paris we flew home to Croydon. Mr Leonard Jackson of Air Work, Heston, (later to become a director in Richard's company, Warden Aviation), and Richard later went to Morane Saulnier's and rebuilt the aircraft then flew it back to Old Warden. It is still in the Shuttleworth Collection.

I was taught to fly by Talbot Lehmann at Chelmsford. He ran a sort of air circus with Billy Burnside. One of my first flights was from the airfield at Colchester, where the Chief Instructor was a man called Bill Goodyear. I later did some dual with him in a Blackburn Bluebird, a side-by-side seater and a dangerous little devil it was. This was the light two-seater biplane designed and built by Blackburn Aeroplane and Motor Co Ltd of Leeds, for the Lympne competitions. This type of aircraft was more convenient for school work than those with tandem seats.

You had to pass certain tests to get your licence, and I obtained mine in 1931. Talbot eventually skipped the country, owing various people money, and left a 504K Avro pegged out on the field at Chelmsford, which he didn't own incidentally. Pat Preston, an Irishman who was at Crompton Parkinson's and who had been interested in flying, told Richard about the Avro. As far as we could see, it was perfectly all right and we got the engine running to experiment with the mixture control

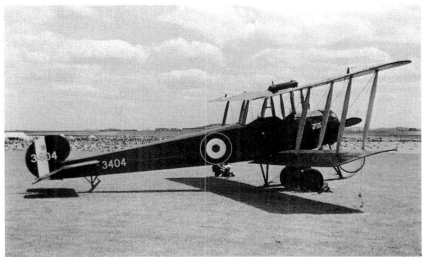

AVRO 504K which dates back to 1915. Purchased by Richard Shuttleworth to be used to provide joy rides for the public. Flown by Jimmy Edmunds between Luton and Dunstable for this purpose.

until we were satisfied we knew the position when the engine would run under maximum power, and later took some castor oil and petrol and filled it up. Pat climbed into the back and I flew it around the countryside. We used this aircraft to take members of the public up for joyrides, at five shillings for five minutes. It was also used, I believe, in the making of the film "Reach for the Sky" in the late 1930s, the life story of Group Captain Douglas Bader.

After the final year of my engineering course, spent with Crompton Parkinson's at Chelmsford, I was wondering what to do with myself when Richard told me where I could buy an aeroplane for £8. We flew over to Henlow to see this aircraft which was owned by Ft. Lt. Allan Wheeler (later Air Commodore) who was stationed at Henlow in 1931/32. He was very helpful to Richard and myself. He was, at the time, building a small single-seater aircraft which he called "The Slymph". I then bought the wreckage of the ANEC II which had no engine, undercarriage or propellor, and which was being used as a rubbish bin. Richard arranged for its removal to Old Warden and I spent all day every day rebuilding it.

The ANEC II bought and re-built by Jimmy Edmunds.

Mrs Shuttleworth kindly invited me to stay on whilst working on this project, and treated me like a second son before G-EBJO was ready to fly.

The ANEC II was designed to take part in the Light Aircraft Trials at Lympne in Kent, in 1924, and was built by the Air Navigation and Engineering Co. Ltd. of Addlestone, Surrey. It was designed by W.S. Shackleton who was the father of Keith Shackleton, the well-known painter of birds and wildlife.

> *The ANEC II was originally fitted with a two-cylinder Anzani engine. It was flown by Jimmy James in the trials in September 1924. The aircraft passed its transport test without problems but trouble began when it was time to fly the ANEC, as it performed reasonably well with one person aboard, but refused to leave the ground with two, which was the whole point of the competition. It was discovered that one cylinder had no compression and when it was dismantled a broken valve was found to be the culprit. Still the ANEC refused to take off, even when the propellor was changed, and after further work and the fitting of a new carburettor, was dragged out for another try. After taking three hours to start, the Anzani finally performed, amid a deafening racket. But, alas, it was too late: the ANEC had already been eliminated because of the troublesome engine. In actual fact, all but seven of the competition's entrants were eliminated through some kind of engine trouble.*
>
> (Ultralights – The Early British Classics, Richard Riding, published by Patrick Stephens Ltd., an imprint of Haynes Publishing, Sparkford, Yeovil, Somerset BA22 7JJ).

The previous engine fitted to the ANEC was a Cherub III and the aircraft was a two-seater. I was walking round the

Air Work workshops at Heston when I came across what appeared to be an almost new ABC Scorpion engine, which had been removed from the Navarro Safety Aircraft. I offered John Parks (later Managing Director of Alvis Car Co. and also a member of 601 Squadron at Hendon) £25 for it, which he accepted. It was heavier than the Bristol Cherub so the ANEC became a single seater.

A little later I walked over the airfield to see Nick Comper (of the Comper Aircraft Co., of which Richard was also a Director). Over the door to his office was a "Fairey Reed" metal propellor. As I went in I said to Nick "That looks as if it would do for my aircraft" and he replied that it was made for an ABC Scorpion engine. "That's what I want it for" I said, and we then agreed that he would sell it to me for a fiver. I was both amazed and grateful.

Having bought the ANEC II, I spent all day every day rebuilding it and this was a tremendously useful period of my life. Its restoration taught me so much about AID procedure and the staff at the Royal Aircraft Establishment at Farnborough were extremely helpful to me, and checked my drawings of the new engine mountings and the undercarriage fittings. As it had no engine or engine mountings and no undercarriage, I bought most of the steel required for remaking those items from R. J. Coley, the celebrated aviator who was also a scrap dealer, in Kingston. The engine mountings were made out of old Jupiter mountings and cut down and redesigned, and the rest were made out of laminations of mild steel, but of an aircraft quality. I drew all that out and made the bits and eventually assembled it. Richard and L. A. Jackson helped me with re-covering and doping the wings, until eventually the great day arrived when all was ready for the flight.

Mr Jarvis, the AID inspector, suggested that Ft/Lt Wheeler should do the first flight, but I thought to myself "not likely" and so when all was ready I opened the throttle and flew over to Henlow. She was a bit nose-heavy, as the Scorpion was heavier than the Cirrus engine originally fitted. Next day I motored over to Henlow to meet Jarvis, who did not realise that I had flown the ANEC over the evening before. Allan Wheeler then proceeded to make the official Test Flight.

The ANEC was a marvellous little aircraft. My younger brother and I kept a small yacht at North Farnbridge on the river Crouch in Essex. I used to fly down from de Havilland's at Stag Lane, Edgeware, where I was working for my Ground Engineer's Licences, and land on the marshes at Farnbridge, spend the weekend sailing and fly back to Stag Lane in time for work on Monday morning. The ANEC would take off in a little over two hundred yards and sit down in not much more.

One story I think would amuse you, I used to fly down to Lymington and land in a field belonging to Col. Bobby Mears. The "ANEC:Scorpion" liked a rich mixture to start. One morning at Lymington I had forgotten to put in a bit of rag to soak with petrol, and which was stuffed in the engine air intake. I took my sock off and this performed the function. Bobby Mears never forgot the incident!

After I had been living at Old Warden for some time, building the ANEC, I began to feel that I was "scrounging" on the good nature and kindness of the Shuttleworth family. I told Richard I thought it was time I "got qualified", then joined the De Havilland Technical School at Stag Lane, Edgware, Middlesex, the Principal of which was a Mr Reeve. I couldn't have done anything better. The whole of the de Havilland family became great personal friends and were very kind and helpful in setting me on my way. And so, in 1934 I obtained my first Commercial Pilot's Licence. De Havilland was a wonderful experience. Hubert Broad was the Chief Test Pilot. Another was Geordie Gibbons and also John de Havilland. Geoffrey de Havilland became Chief Test Pilot and Hubert went to Brockworth with Hawkers. Unfortunately both the de Havillands and Geordie Gibbons were killed flying. Geordie and John collided in the air and were killed. Geoffrey was attempting to go through the sound barrier and

Autographed photo of Geoffrey de Havilland seated in a BE3.

he lost his life when the engine broke loose and killed him. An absolute tragedy.

One of the most extraordinary and amusing things occurred when I eventually decided to get a Commercial Pilot's Licence and I had never been in the air before at night. I flew down to Croydon and wanted night flying dual. I met Max Findlay, an Instructor at Brooklands, at 8pm, as arranged and he took the front seat, I the back, and he told me to fly to Talsfield, which was about twenty miles. We went around it and back to Croydon. I landed it and we got out and he said "You're all right, so you can go on to Lympne". That brief encounter was the only night flying dual in my life! There was a beacon at Penshurst which I passed on the way and cloud came lower and lower. Much to my relief, in front of me was the beacon at Lympne and I was able to complete my test for the Commercial Pilot's Licence.

After obtaining my Commercial Pilot's licence and Ground Engineer's licences I had no time to fly the ANEC. Very reluctantly I sold dear G-EBJO to a South African.

Unfortunately I let him have all the drawings I had made of the engine mountings and undercarriage fittings, etc. I am happy to know that the remains of this aircraft have now fortunately come to roost in the Shuttleworth Collection and that the aircraft will once again be restored, and put on display.

When I obtained my Desoutter Commercial Pilot's Licence Richard loaned me an aircraft fitted with a Gypsy 3 engine – GAAZI – and as Richard was a Director of the Comper Aircraft Company and had a factory in the corner of Heston, I was able to, at least for a time, house my aircraft in Nick Comper's hangar. It was the Comper Aircraft Company established at Hooton Park, Cheshire, which produced the Comper Swift which Richard flew to India in 1933, some six

Will Hawkes, Chairman (left) and David Reader, Hon. Sec. of 'Prop Swing' journal of the Shuttleworth Veteran Aeroplane Society the support body of the Richard Ormonde Shuttleworth Remembrance Trust, recently unloading the fuselage of the 1924 ANEC II G-EBJO on arrival at Old Warden from the Kingshill barn. Courtesy: 'Prop Swing'.

thousand miles in around twelve days. Richard and Flight Lieutenant Nick Comper were Directors. Nigel Norman (later Sir Nigel, PA to the Duke of Kent) was one of the founders of Heston Airport. He was very helpful to me when I first started flying commercially, and used to invite me to his house and he and his wife Patricia were both extremely kind and helpful. I soon made friends with Joe Birkett who ran an air charter business, mostly for the benefit of the Press. Joe gave me my first commercial flight, carrying a passenger, and we remained very firm friends to the day he died. This flight was to Selsey Bill and if I remember correctly, the passenger was Sir Anthony Lindsey Hogg. I was a freelance charter pilot, – never worked for an airline. We used to do a lot of work for the Press. I then got together with a distinguished American lawyer, Douglas Gibbs and his wife who was the daughter of Hubert Hartigan, a race-horse trainer, and we started running services to race meetings. We went to all the principal English races, sometimes landing on the course, or in an adjacent field. In 1938 we carried nearly three thousand people racing.

I joined the Reserve of Airforce Officers in 1934, not entirely out of patriotic duty, but because I wished to have access to a Link trainer in order to bring my instrument flying up to a high level, which I was able to do. Later on the Air Ministry wrote to me as someone had recommended me for the Air Efficiency Award. They had previously suggested that I should leave the Reserve of Airforce Officers and join the Volunteer Reserve, but as I had been perfectly satisfied in the Reserve of Airforce Officers I replied that the arrangement I had made in 1934 had been perfectly satisfactory as far as I was concerned and if it was no longer so, would they erase my name. They in turn replied that they were happy for me to remain in the Reserve of Airforce Officers for the duration of my time with them, but I was informed that I would not be eligible for the Air Efficiency Award as it was only awarded for the Volunteer Reserve, the RAFVR!

It was at Eton that Richard was taught the basics of mechanical engineering. He developed an interest in motorcars – in addition to aircraft – and became a very successful motor rally and racing driver, his motor racing career culminating in the winning of the British Grand Prix at Donington Park in 1935, when he drove his 2.5 litre Alfa Romeo Monoposto. This was probably his greatest love. He established a motor racing workshop at Brooklands, which had the reputation of being the premier racing circuit in England during the inter-war period. Richard purchased his first aeroplane in 1931 and learned to fly for expediency no doubt. Nevertheless, he courageously participated in the Viceroy of India Cup Contest in 1933, when he flew solo to India, and was placed fourth.

Richard Shuttleworth was a keen conservationist and a man of vision, who began collecting and restoring cars in 1928 and aeroplanes from 1935. After inheriting the Old Warden Estate, he developed his interests in agriculture, forestry and estate management and became President of the Bedfordshire Agricultural Society in 1935.

Richard was sadly killed in an aircraft accident in 1940, and shortly afterwards, his mother established the Trust.

The Shuttleworth years were for me the happiest, most glorious and stupendous times that any young man could imagine, let alone live through.'

JIMMY EDMUNDS

Richard Shuttleworth – Chronology

June 1930	Competes with Jimmy Edmunds in "Old Crocks Race" at Brooklands in De Dietrich, lapping at 75mph
28 Apr 1932	Edmunds and Shuttleworth – G-EBWD – 1hr 30min from Hatfield
6 May 1932	Edmunds and Shuttleworth – G-EBWD – Croydon–Villacouble
12 Aug 1932	With Edmunds in Hermes II Moth G-EBUF – Chelmsford–Ashwell

16 Aug 1932	With Edmunds in Hermes II Moth – G-EBUF – Ashwell–Liverpool
22 Aug 1932	With Edmunds in G-EBUF – Hooton–Leighton Buzzard–Heston
25 Aug 1932	With Edmunds in G-EBWD – Brooklands–Hamble–Old Sarum–Winchester–Brooklands
11 Nov 1932	With Edmunds in G-EBWD – Lympne–St. Ingelvert–"Landed on beach at Boulogne"
13 Nov 1932	With Edmunds flying G-EBWD – Lympne–Leighton Buzzard–Old Warden
28 Dec 1932	With Edmunds in G-EBWD – Old Warden–Brooklands (40 minutes)–Hanworth–Old Warden
4 Jan 1933	With Edmunds in G-EBWD – Farnborough–Brooklands–Leighton Buzzard–Old Warden
7 Mar 1933	With Edmunds flying G-EBWD – Hatfield–Lympne–Abbeville–Lympne–Broxbourne–Old Warden
10 Mar 1933	With Edmunds flying G-EBWD – Warden–Brooklands
15 Mar 1933	With Edmunds in G-EBWD – Old Warden–Hooton
16 Mar 1933	With Edmunds in G-EBWD – Hooton–Sywell–Riseley–Old Warden
17 Mar 1933	With Edmunds in G-EBWD – Old Warden–Milton Ernest–Old Warden
21 Apr 1933	With Edmunds in G-EBWD – Heston–Lympne–Le Bourget–Lyon
22 Apr 1933	With Edmunds in G-EBWD – Lyon–Marseilles ("very strong tail wind – averaged 125mph!") –Nice
17 Jan 1934	Edmunds flies Pobjoy Swift G-ABWE from Old Warden to Sywell, with "Richard in Desoutter"
14 Jan 1934	With Edmunds flying Desoutter – G-AAPS. Around Heston
18 Jan 1934	With Edmunds in G-AAPS – Speke–Hooton–Old Warden ("Overshot Old Warden and found ourselves at Ashwell. Windows rather dirty!")
12 Feb 1934	With Edmunds in Desoutter G-AAPS – Lympne–St. Ingelvert
13 Feb 1934	With Edmunds in Desoutter G-AAPS – St. Ingelvert–Abbeville–St. Quentin–Commercy
15 July 1934	With Edmunds –Desoutter G-AAZI (Gipsy III) – Old Warden–Croydon

FINAL OVERVIEWS

FINAL OVERVIEWS

A Lutonian Reminisces

Wootton & Webb, Chemists.
Photo: Luton & Neighbourhood Illustrated. Pub. T G Hobbs.

'*My grandfather was a chemist in Dunstable and later at Wootton and Webb pharmacy. He then had his own shop in Brunswick Street. He moved from Houghton Regis to Luton while my father was still young. My father often used to meet him from work and it was very seldom that he saw any vehicle on the road between Luton and Dunstable – just the miller's waggon and carrier's cart which plied between Luton and Dunstable two days a week. The route was a dark lane from the area where Dunstable Road begins in the centre of Luton, up to Dunstable Road, with high hedges and overhanging trees. Father was frightened of going along this lane at night during winter, but when the light evenings came he would go to meet his father.*

My mother lived to be little short of a hundred and has now been dead some thirty years. I was born when she was about forty-five. What she and father told me goes back many years. They lived in Houghton Regis before they married. My mother used to walk from Houghton Regis to the centre of Luton each day before she married, and worked a twelve hour day, starting at 6am. I believe she was a machinist then. She made this walk every day, and there were few buildings there then, just a laundry at the top of Beech Hill. The Gas Works had been built at this time, and Christ Church at the top of George Street, was in the process of being built.

The first business in Luton to have electricity installed was a business on Park Square. My father stood as a young man and watched, with the place packed with people, waiting to see the light switched on. A high proportion of the population of Luton waited there to see the electric light switched on. There was a pond on the square at that time. [In 1920 less than a million people in Britain had electricity and millions were without running water. By 1939 nine million people had electricity and over 80% of homes had running water.]

There were other isolated incidents related by my father, such as when King Edward VII came and there was a meeting in the Assembly Hall and the Mayor opened the meeting with the words "Me and the King"!

It was not uncommon to see cattle being driven in the street, for slaughter. The large open air market with canvas canopies and naphtha flares after dark was a remarkable sight. Something of the character was lost when the market was moved indoors.

My father was a blocker in the hat trade and for seventeen years he worked for Harts hat manufacturers, and was apprenticed to them. I was born when he was quite elderly. He left Harts and started as a traveller on his own, as a salesman and peddler of hats. He travelled around by train and my mother told me that after he bought his three-monthly season ticket, there was often little profit left.

The hat trade was susceptible to fire. There was one in Cheapside in which several women were burned to death. There was another in Bridge Street. Another big fire in the town during the First World War was at Lyes Dye Factory in Old Bedford Road near the entrance to People's Park. It occurred during the night. This was because extremely combustible materials were used – straw, varnishes and so on. There were several big dye works. Hubbards were contributors to the hat trade. With supporting trades the hat business was probably substantial, with many people involved. There was a lot of piece-work and home-work done. Many women worked part-time and there were many family businesses on the go. How they compared in numbers we do not know but the engineering trades must have caught up very quickly. Fashion eventually changed and men and women ceased to wear hats. At one time men wore straw hats with a wide brim in Luton. Six or seven policemen were permitted to wear straw helmets during the summer months, the same shape as the Bobby's hat, with a badge on the front, but made of straw and identifiable from the policeman's usual helmet.

Years ago when you walked through Luton, you could hear the machines going in people's houses. A lot of work was taken out to girls at home and collected on Fridays. My mother was a machinist in the hat trade. Many people were employed in the hat trade, but figures were over-estimated compared with those employed in engineering.

About 1905 the Vauxhall Iron Company moved to Luton from London and they were probably the biggest employers in the town. From this time other large firms began to appear, including SKF, Commer Cars Company and George Kent. There were many large hat factories and many small semi-household businesses, with the business in the back yard, but from an early time the engineering industry was overtaking employment in the hat trade.

George Street was the important shopping area. For years Woolworths sold goods priced at 3d or 6d. Marks and Spencer sold nothing over a penny, but this changed, probably by the time of the first war. They used to display a notice to this effect. High Town shops were popular with people living in the area, in the streets between High Town Road and Hitchin Road.

There was a disparity between Dunstable and Luton. For many years local land-owners did not want the railway and would not sell land for this purpose. When Dunstable was

George Street, Luton, with the Town Hall in the background. The scene of business activity, it was congested by traffic and required 'efficient regulation on the part of police officers'. This photograph was taken prior to the introduction of the trams.
Photo: Luton & Neighbourhood Illustrated. Pub. T G Hobbs.

still a little town, Luton was a large and thriving industrial place.

Leagrave was a separate village. Later there was a lot of ribbon building, with houses on both sides of the road. Leagrave became joined on to Luton eventually. At the end of the First World War it was regarded as a separate village and not within the Borough of Luton.

The Gas Works was in Crawley Road, in a populated area, where you could smell gas over half of the town! It was used for cooking and for street lighting, with lamplighters who used their hook-ons to light the lamps. At the end of the first war it was used for street lighting and for the majority of private houses. Some must have been in existence after the Second World War!

The Corn Exchange was used for the exchange of grain, but the area was not a well-known corn growing area and the Corn Exchange had diminished in importance by the First World War.

The temperance stranglehold was strong in Luton: magistrates and members of the Luton Town Council were

'Franklin' Temperance and Commercial Hotel near Luton Town Hall. Photo: Luton & Neighbourhood Illustrated. Pub. T G Hobbs.

drawn substantially from the nonconformist element in the town and were strict on the subject of temperance and drink. Gradually the nonconformity of the town came into different hands and very different magistrates sat on the bench. At one time the Rev. Joshua Holmes, Superintendent Methodist Minister, published an article in the Luton News condemning the magistrates for allowing what he described as a "great ring of drinking palaces". This was a reference to the inns at Kingsway and Halfway House. It was a vast change from what the town had previously known.'

CLAUDE HORWOOD

A Dunstablian Reminisces

'At the turn of the century, as it had been earlier, Dunstable was very much a country market town and in fact it continued in this vein for at least another fifty years.

Although there was a little industry, Dunstable was really a town of shops and shopkeepers and as the great majority of the tradesmen lived over and behind their shops their public life and their private life and their social life were in the town itself. They did not shut up their shops at night and disappear into the country and return to open them the next morning. There was very little commuting; what there was was to the hat trade in Luton (although Dunstable still had its share of hat factories and bonnet rooms and block making sheds), so as a result there was a good community spirit.

This was added to by the large churches of the town – the ancient Priory, the big Wesleyan Methodist church at The Square, the big Baptist church close by in West Street, the Congregational chapel down Edward Street and the Primitive Methodist building in Victoria Street. Their big days such as Harvest Festival, the Church Anniversary and above all the Sunday School Anniversary, when there was often a parade through the streets, were marked as part of the town's life and were faithfully recorded in great detail in the pages of the Dunstable Borough Gazette. As well as the churches the Grammar School (Dunstable School), which was opened in 1888, in High Street North, played a prominent part within the context of the town – it was very much "town and gown". The school helped the town events, the town supported school affairs and actively took note of the school's big days.

The hub of Dunstable was the cross roads, with the policeman on point duty, where the two famous roads, the ancient British Icknield Way and the Roman Watling Street met, as they do today. But from that centre radiated the strength and purpose of the town and numerous shops spread out along the two High Streets, West Street and Church Street. The entrance and exit of the last-named road is the only one that has really changed in size over recent years, when the narrow street was widened by the demolition of the old Red Lion Hotel on one corner and the Home & Colonial Stores and Freeman, Hardy & Willis opposite.

These shops served not only Dunstable itself, but the villages and hamlets round about. The village folk came into the "big town" for nearly all their wares – groceries and greengroceries, meat, clothing, floor coverings, bedding, pills and medicines, games and sports wear, confectionery, ironmongery, etc. They came in the early days by walking, on horseback, or by pony and trap or carrier wagon. Then perhaps by bicycle and as the motor vehicle came into their lives by the bus, often only running on market days.

On market days there was much activity in Dunstable. On Wednesday and Saturday the open stalls of the market, lit in winter by naphtha flares, stretched from the corner of West Street, along the face of the old Town Hall and sometimes spilling on to the High Street, to the corner of Albion Street, opposite the Sugar Loaf Hotel. Then there was the Cattle Market on The Square, twice weekly up to the last war, thence once per week, when all was hustle and bustle with the animals and poultry and farmers and carts and vans and the auctioneer, and of course the hangers-on. Sometimes hustle and bustle turned to frenzied activity when an animal escaped or hens got loose and those responsible hurtled around trying to rescue their charges. There were also pens down in Tavistock Street in the northern end of the town and on a Sunday afternoon or evening the farmers from Hockliffe and round about would drive their cattle up the Chalk Cutting into these pens, where the livestock was then herded into railway cattle trucks and despatched to various destinations. The drive up the Chalk Cutting was watched as a weekly ritual and many are the stories told over this adventure.

Apart from half a dozen or so multiple stores, all the shops were individually owned and all had the owner's name on the fascia. The multiples, only a fraction of the size of today's big stores, included the International Stores, World Stores, the aforementioned Home & Colonial and Freeman, Hardy & Willis, the Co-op, and two or three meat chains. But what is so interesting is that apart from the variety – there was really no need to go anywhere else than Dunstable to shop – was the number of shops of the same category. At the end of the 1930s for instance, there were twenty-two butcher's shops scattered around the town, and going back to 1914 when the population of Dunstable was around seven thousand, there were, amongst other, 14 butchers, 24 grocers and provision merchants, 5 greengrocers, 10 bakers, 9 confectioners, 6 fishmongers, 12 drapers, 8 tailors, 11 nurserymen and florists, 15 representatives of the boot and shoe trade, 7 coal merchants, 7 hairdressers and 31 names classified under the title of shopkeeper (Kelly's Directory, 1914). Some of these were in back streets and side streets, of course, but those and the High Street shops all served a particular community. These records are probably typical of good sized country market towns up and down the land in the first part of the century, and like Dunstable, they probably all had characters and personalities. Certainly Dunstable did, many of them, and Dunstable also had its own character, its own individuality.

This character was also helped by some of the buildings, including some large houses with big gardens where doctors and dentists practised. The former Town Hall, looking rather like a Great Western railway station in front and with a magnificent four-sided clock, was a character building and served Dunstable well and fully. It was often the venue and scene of town events. Saturday night "hops", concerts, poultry shows, flower shows, cinematograph displays, church bazaars, whist drives, town meetings, rallies, celebratory teas and lunches, the list is almost endless. Election results were given out from the balcony, the crowd waiting below. The deliberations of the Town Council took place at the back in the Council Chamber. The Fire Engine was stored in a shed behind the Town Hall. Some of the heart went out of the town when the Town Hall was unceremoniously demolished in 1966.

There were lots or organisations and clubs in the town, as well as those connected with the life of the churches. Sporting and social clubs abounded and of the former the Town cricket and bowls clubs enjoyed a high reputation. There were mid-week teams for football and cricket as well as the Saturday matches, as early closing on a Thursday afternoon was the rule except for a few cafés and the big banks. The Literary & Scientific Society was of a high calibre, packing the Town Hall for their winter meetings, often addressed by eminent and well-known speakers. The Three Arts company and the Operatic & Dramatic Society put on regular shows, often in the Palace Cinema, where the Post Office now stands, but there were many smaller clubs, all of which had their devotees.

Traffic in the High Street, before motor cars and motor bikes and buses and lorries thundering through at night, centred around the horse, and even right up to the Second World War, horses were still used. There were farm carts and pony and traps a-plenty, big horses pulled the coal carts from the two stations, where the coal merchants had their individual sidings from the trains, and delivered coal around the town. The station horses and carts trundled to and fro delivering items and then there were the brewers drays from Bennett's Brewery on the corner of Chiltern Road and High Street North. Milk was often brought in from the village farms in tall churns by horse and cart and there were bakers who delivered bread by small covered wagon. With all this horse traffic there were a lot of droppings in the streets, but the Council employed a man to come along with bucket and spade. Dunstable was a clean town – the gutters were swept every morning and the shop keepers washed their frontage down at least twice a week, so that it was clean for their customers and general pedestrians to walk on. The curse of chewing gum had not yet arrived, but in any case, litter was not dropped on the streets. In those days that was part of the unwritten law of discipline.

At the beginning of the narrative mention was made of a little industry. Waterlow & Sons (printing), Bagshawe's and Harrison Carter (engineering) and Cross & Co. (table paperware) were the main employers and they gave impetus and a certain security to the town. A. C. Sphinx (sparking plugs) was to join them in 1934 and open up the northern end of the town. But Dunstable was unique in some other trades of a smaller nature. The Flemons family were herbalists and many Dunstable folk, children and adults, used to go out into the surrounding countryside and pick blossoms and berries and roots, in return for payment from the Flemons. Mr J. T. Dales manufactured his world famous Dales' Dubbin from a tiny factory and yard. [The Dunstable & District Local History Society in 1995 held two very successful evenings when they presented some of the old trades of Dunstable. It is their intention to publish a series of booklets on these trades and the first one will be produced in 1996, on "Dales' Dubbin and Flemons' Herbs".] And on the edges of the town or what, at one time, were the edges, were five Whiting works for the production of whiting for cleansing and other purposes, extracted from the local chalk. Here again horses and carts would bring the chalk from small quarries to the whiting sheds and vats at the corner of Meadway (where the lane leads up to the Golf Course) to the corner of Green Lanes (opposite the lower slopes of the Downs), to the top of Beale Street, to the corner of Victoria Street and Chiltern Road and to the back of Bennett's Rec. where it meets Bull Pond Lane. All gone now, but once a thriving industry and part of old Dunstable this century.

But also part of the town's life at that time were the people who wandered into the town. Thus there was the muffin man, with a big wooden flat tray full of muffins on his head, held by one hand whilst he rang a bell with his free hand, crying out as he went along "Muffins, muffins!" Also the shrimp seller, with a tray full of shrimps and a tin pottle in which they were measured. But every day at dusk came the town's lamplighter, with a long pole with a hook on its end, to light the gas lamps in the main roads and the back streets.

These people generally walked everywhere. But many Dunstablians walked, too, and Sunday evening on a fine summer's day was promenade time. Up and down the High Street, yes, but particularly West Street, with its tree-bordered road and past the Cemetery and meadows to the bottom of the Downs and the beginning of Green Lanes, which were a great perambulation stretch. The local folk made use of the lovely country on the edge of the town – walking along the top of the Chalk Cutting with the cornfields stretching down to Houghton Regis; straight along the Green Lanes to Totternhoe and Sewell (farmers still drove their sheep along these lanes, the drovers ways); over the fields to Kensworth, all three of these walks before quarries desecrated the scene. And, of course, to the top of the Downs, to look at the magnificent view and gently stroll along the ridge or sit down on one of the old wooden plank seats.

There are many, many other things that could be said about "Old Dunstable", but space does not permit. These are my memories, shared by many others, and in some cases learnt from earlier generations, in the time-honoured way of being "handed down".'

COLIN BOURNE

A Bedfordian Reminisces

'I was born in Elthorne Road, Holloway, but came to Bedford as a child with my parents. My father moved here to manage Eastman's Butchers in St. Mary's, but we later established our own business – Woods Butchers – in Harrowden Road.

The area south of the river is very well known to me and this area has changed so much in my lifetime. It used to be a thriving commercial area, with numerous small businesses. There must have been two hundred people came off the train each morning, going to business or school. The Bletchley line. I can tell you every shop from here to the water bridge – and beyond.

There was Turner's the rope people, then the pub kept by the Fosters [Railway Swan], over the other side of the road from the station that was. Opposite there was Wollason, a vet, then Palmer's Fish Shop and Palmer's Fruit Shop, then a tobacconist. Wilmer's Butchers was on the corner, and coming towards the hospital, Morris the barber, Sadd the butcher, then Hester's Cake Shop. Where the roundabout is on the corner there was a pub called The Goat and next door Damon the fruiterer and another pub called The Phoenix. This is St. John's. Then Walter's grocer, Miss Frodson, music. In her back garden was a vet named Allen. Curruthers the chemist, The Pig and Whistle pub, then Blakeman's the fruiterer, Alan Smith's pub, then a paper shop called Stevens, run by mother and son. Next there was a yard at the back with about four or five horses, then another Blakeman's, fruiterer's shop, then the pub which is still there, and Wilsons, which sold carpets and so on. Eastman's butchers and then a pub on the corner, The Olney Arms.

On the other side of the road, [St. John's Street, east side], Turner's the rope people had a shop near The George. Brightman's sold bicycles. There were two shops belonging to Mrs Wright, sweets, then Impey's the dairy, then a high-class tailor, then the flower shop. Hill's Butchers shop – there were sixteen this side of the bridge! Then a herbalist, then a pub on the corner [The Fountain].

In St. Mary's [Street, west side] the first shop on the left was a tailor named Heath, then a little gown shop, then Daniels the butcher. Wilson's Garage and a corner café, big man's clothes shop, Cox & Harpur, and then a yard went up the back, wholesale bricks and mortar and things like that. Boots Chemist, and Halford's cycle shop.

On the other side of the road [St. Mary's Street, east side], the first shop was Goodman's, sports outfitters, a pub which is still there [King's Arms], Randall's and a shoe repairer [Lansberry]. Next St. Mary's Post Office, Stevens grocers, a motor cycle shop belonging to Sid Crawley. Then there was a path went down to the back, then a big dress shop, all the ladies went there [John Bates], and then there was a walk down to the boats: the operator's were called Chethams. That's where the Picturedrome was, overlooking the river.

John Bates Outfitters.
Photo: Mates Illustrated Guide to Bedford, 1906.

Now Cauldwell Street, on the left side was the Olney Arms and the Westminster Bank, then the back entrance to Wilson's where the carpets were cleaned, then a garage which operated on the other side of the road as well. They made carts and all sorts of things. They didn't sell petrol. On the other side was just repairs to various vehicles, mostly traders' vehicles. Then the vicarage, St. Mary's, then a pub – on both sides of an alleyway.

On the left-hand side, continuing, was Dudeney and Johnston and on the other side of the road a hairdresser's. A hair cut then used to be about 4d. Next was a pub, where Nicholls was the publican. They also did a grocery round in the villages. Then a Butcher, Coleman, then a cycle shop, Kings, then a butcher, Martin & Sharp.

On the other side of the road [Cauldwell Street] before Nutting's, was St. Mary's School Room, then Nutting's Corn Chandlers sold everything including bird seed. After Nutting's a shop which repaired car radiators. Then the Cherry Tree pub. Up the back of it there was stables for all Franklins Coal Merchants' horses. After the pub there was a famous man, harness maker called Pearson. Big church – Moravian possible [Methodist Chapel] and on the corner a fruit shop, Mantons, then Circuit the undertaker. On the next corner and just round it, Burnapp's fish and chip shop. After than Benson's one of the best butchers in the town, where they made sausages with all the best meat and people queued for them. Their pigs were killed at Wilstead at the Ivy Lane slaughterhouse run by Mr Smith. After Benson's a grocer's shop and then cobbler, then the Black Diamond pub [now the site of County Hall].

Now the High Street. On the corner was Murkett's the garage at the side of the Swan Hotel. Then a dress shop, Wells' furniture shop, Bithrey's tobacconist [known as Luddingtons]. Next [after Bull's Passage] Baccus, garden tools, hardware, cake shop, The Rose pub, jewellers who are the Rolex agents, Curry's electrical, chemist, Taylor, Brawn &

High Street.
Photo: Mates Illustrated Guide to Bedford, 1906.

Flood, which was on the corner of Mill Street and the High Street. There used to be a cinema called the Palace on the opposite corner, as a matter of interest. Next a classy gown shop, then the bank, greengrocer, then a passageway. Teeth repairs – which closed only two years ago – then Goldings.

Enough for now, but I could go on. I can see it all now, in my mind's eye.'

RICHARD 'DICKY' WOOD

EPILOGUE

Social History is a subject which fascinates the writer, and one which has attracted an explosion of interest by academics and others over recent decades. Research into family history is now a preoccupation of multitudes. Articles are appearing everywhere to enlighten and enthral enthusiastic readers and illuminate the changing nature of lifestyles throughout the last century in particular. After decades of technological innovation, economic prosperity and improving living conditions (in relative terms), many questions are now being raised about damage to the environment in particular, caused by the demands of the lifestyle we lead. In addition to becoming environmentally aware, many are now recognising the frustration of life in a society which is orientated towards egocentricity and greed.

A nostalgia for things past would tend to indicate a certain measure of dissatisfaction with prevailing social conditions. Perhaps only now are we beginning to challenge the inevitability of twentieth century urbanised lifestyles, and are endeavouring to create for ourselves a situation where we can have greater control over our lives and destinies. In contemplation of a more spiritually enriching way of life, perhaps we should be mindful of the lessons which the past has to offer.

I owe a great debt to so many kind people who have contributed to my books. Those who survive to publication of the series will, I hope, feel that I have dealt sympathetically with the material at my disposal, and have portrayed the cause as faithfully as possible.

I trust that all who have read these books of mine, concerned as they are with the lives of Bedfordshire people, – an important part of our heritage – will have enjoyed the experience, and may themselves feel inspired to further investigation and personal enrichment.

Brenda Fraser-Newstead

CONTRIBUTORS

WINIFRED LOUISA ALLAN (NÉE HODBY)

Winnie was born at Knotting Green on 8 January 1919. Her father and his father were also born there, in a tied cottage near the church. Her father spent all his working life on Green Farm, owned by Mr Pike. There were no privately owned properties in the village at that time. Of the six children born to Winnie's parents, one died at the age of twelve with appendicitis.

Winnie's family have always been active church members. Her grandfather was an organist and her father too, both self-taught. One vicar (Rev. Wiggins) looked after two parishes then, Knotting and Souldrop. Most village people were church-goers and at harvest festival and the Knotting Feast the church would be packed to capacity.

Winnie met her husband in Bedford in 1938. He was in the Airforce training at Cardington, but he came from Scotland. He was posted to Mildenhall but they kept in touch and were married on New Year's Eve, 1941. As a time-serving airman, he saw action in the Second World War, and was invalided out in 1944.

MAURICE CHARLES BOYLES

Maurice was born in Marston on 7 October 1928 at his maternal grandmother's home. The family moved to Wootton where he attended Wootton School until the age of fourteen, and remained in Wootton until his marriage at the age of twenty-four to a girl from Cranfield. He worked for his father after leaving school, and took over the business when his father retired in 1968. After his marriage he moved to Cranfield and has lived in the same house since 1955.

He hopes to remain there for the rest of his days.

FREDA ELIZABETH BROWN (NÉE COOKE)

Freda was born on 15 April 1914, at 53 Russell Street, Bedford, the eldest of five children. Her father was in the 11th and 13th Hussars, and he married her mother in 1910.

Freda's parents were both Bedfordians, and her father worked at the gas works in Queens Park for most of his life, but there were times when he was out of work, and her mother then went out waitressing at the County Club near the Swan Hotel.

GEORGE WILLIAM BROWN

George was born in Aylesbury in December 1913. His father, a member of the 1st Bedfordshire Regiment 5th division (L/C Brown, Signaller), was born in Norfolk but of Scottish descent. His mother came from Northampton originally.

After repatriation, George's parents made their home in Foster Hill Road, Bedford. He attended the Harpur Trust Elementary School from the age of four.

George was involved in a motor accident on St. John's Bridge in 1937, in which he sustained multiple injuries, and at the age of sixty-two, was involved in an industrial accident, in which he was badly injured. He received no compensation for either accident, and one feels that he is the innocent victim of his circumstances. He has suffered greatly throughout his life in terms of physical pain and mental anguish. His wife Freda has been a great support and loyal companion to him for over fifty years.

JOHN FREDERICK BUCKLEDEE

John was born on 22 August 1910 in Lindsey, Suffolk. His father was a farm worker whose job on the farm was the care of the shire horses. John was brought up in a thatched cottage, in a very agricultural climate. After leaving school he eventually became a footman at Ampthill House, now demolished. He married in 1938 and he and his wife had a son and two daughters. He joined the Dunstable Police Force in 1935, and remained a police officer until his retirement, and continued to work after his official retirement, with the Council, as an Investigations Officer for the Luton Rural District Council, and later for the South Beds District Council, using his knowledge gained as a policeman. Now aged eighty-four, he lives in Preston near Weymouth, close to his daughter, and frequently flies to South Africa to see his other daughter and family. His son is the editor of a local newspaper. He still enjoys a game of bowls and gardening.

FREDERICK BURRAWAY

Fred, one of seven children, was born in 1905 in a cottage in Cause End Road, Wootton, which has since been demolished. His father worked as a Setter for the London Brick Company, then known as Forders Ltd. Fred has lived all his life in the village and has many memories of Wootton and its people, since his early days.

After a two-year courtship, Fred married his wife at the age of twenty-two and took a cottage near the bakehouse where he worked all his life. He has very happy memories of a lifetime spent in the employ of the Juffs family, local bakers, and maintains that given the opportunity he would love to do it all over again.

WINIFRED BURTON (NÉE POULTER)

Winnie was born on 1 October 1909 in Cricket Lane, Bedford, in a thatched cottage which has since disappeared. Her parents moved to School Yard when she was about three, at the back of Barkers Lane and near to Goldington School. Winnie's father was a sheet metal worker at Allens, as was his father. There were three children in the family.

Winnie was married at twenty-four, to a painter, decorator and signwriter, and continued to work only as a holiday relief, until her son was born.

FRANK PERCY CHAPMAN

Frank was born on 3 March 1900 at 31 Ashton Street, Luton, where he lived until he was married at twenty-three. His mother didn't want him to have a motor for the wedding, so he had to get a carriage and pair of greys. Powdrill did the wedding (they were building contractors and had a farm) and as Frank lived only two minutes from the church, they were driven right round the town before actually going into church. Rudds, where his mother worked, did the wedding cake, for which they charged two pounds: Frank thought it was worth five at least! He regarded this as a favour, since they were friends and neighbours.

On the occasion of his Diamond Wedding Anniversary, Frank and his wife received a telegram from the Queen, of which he is very proud.

WILLIAM CONSTANT

Bill's father was born in Bedfordshire, but Bill was born on 29 July 1916 at Hessett, near Bury St. Edmunds, Suffolk, his mother being a Suffolk woman. There were three children in the family, two boys and one girl, but Bill's brother, the last-born of the children, died of meningitis when he was four or five. Bill was nearly five when his parents came to live in Renhold.

EDITH IRENE ELIZABETH CORNWELL (NÉE CROWSLEY)

Edith was born in Dudley Street, Bedford, on 16 February, 1910. Her parents later moved to Bower Street, near the embankment. She has always been known as 'Irene'.

Irene's husband was related to Jack Cornwell VC, who was in the Royal Navy. She and her husband had six children, and she now has sixteen grandchildren and eleven great grandchildren. She has been widowed for twenty-eight years, enjoyed her married life but is now quietly contented and has never wanted to re-marry: thinks she is old-fashioned!

CHRISTOPHER JOHN CREAMER

Chris was born on 14 December 1903 at Church End, Milton Bryan. His father was a woodman/forester on the Woburn Estate. Their home was a charity cottage, belonging to the Milton Bryan Charity. Chris's grandfather, Levi Creamer, worked on Manor Farm, which was part of the Battlesden Estate. His mother played the organ at the local church from the time she was nine years old, and her mother –

grandmother Clark – who had always lived in Milton Bryan, died at the age of 97.

Chris officially retired at 65, but received no pension, and has worked since then for a local farmer, hedging and ditching, and helping with the cows.

JIMMY HENRY EDMUNDS

Jimmy was born in Buckinghamshire in 1909, but lived for many years in Great Staughton, near the Bedfordshire/Cambridgeshire border. He was associated with Bedfordshire in a business capacity, having, among other things, been co-director with Richard Shuttleworth in an advertising venture, the works of which were situated at Old Warden, and having at one time acquired a corn merchanting enterprise in Biggleswade.

Jimmy was a pilot: his first flight was with Richard Shuttleworth in 1931, and this initiation aroused his life-long enthusiasm for flight.

ELSIE ROSE ENGLAND

Elsie was born on 1 July 1905 at 44 High Street South, Dunstable. the property – her parents' home and bakery – was on the corner of High Street South and Britain Street, and the house is now occupied by a firm of accountants.

In her younger days, Elsie worked for a Dunstable firm of herbalists known as Flemons and later called Flemons and Marchant. They employed men to collect dandelion roots, comfry leaves, foxgloves and so on, which were sold to wholesalers for drug houses. They also made their own herbal medicines.

Dunstable was a relatively small place in Elsie's youth, and everybody knew everybody else.

HENRY FARRER

Henry was born on 13 September 1919 at Cranfield. His father, Harry Farrer, had been born at Hall End, Wootton, in 1888. His mother ran a fried fish stall at Hall End in the early nineteen hundreds.

Henry's parents married in 1913 and moved to Cranfield. In 1921 the family moved to a redundant public house which had been called The Old George, in the centre of the village, where they started a fish and chip shop, as there were plenty of rooms and out-houses. They also hawked fish and fruit round Cranfield and the surrounding villages including villages now engulfed within the Milton Keynes development. Henry began work for his father at about the age of ten years, firstly hawking with a basket on his arm, and later with a truck which his father had made with the wheels of an old bath-chair. He and his brother, born in 1921, also helped to cure fish in the backyard, where their father built his own smoke-house.

Henry was the first Cranfield boy to be a Boy Scout (1st North Crawley Troop, 1936). He first started entertaining in 1931/2 and with a few friends, built a form of marionette show which he'd seen described in a book at school. They performed it on the village green to a group of local children and the schoolmaster saw the show and arranged for them to perform it to the whole school of about a hundred and sixty children.

IVY FLUTE (NÉE LAWSON)

Ivy was born on 16 February 1916 at Radwell, a hamlet near Felmersham. Her father was the local rag-and-bone merchant, known as 'Raggy Lawson'.

Ivy's father collapsed and died after a trip to London, in 1950, aged 72. Ivy inherited enough money to send her son to Bedford Modern School and he went on to university and is now a teacher. She remembers her father with admiration and affection.

ARTHUR RICHARD HARVEY

Arthur was born on 14 October 1911 in Greyfriars Walk, Bedford. His father was a boxer at one time, and was for many years a market trader, trading in seafoods.

Arthur has had an assortment of jobs over the years, but only took these to fit in with his boxing interests and to support himself. He spent four years at Robertsons and six years at Allens in Coventry during the war, making aircraft parts and munitions. He was in the Home Guard, the RAF and later the Royal Navy. He joined the Merchant Navy for a time in 1949 and visited Australia twice during this time.

PRUDENCE MARY HEADEY (NÉE THODY)

Prudence was born on 24 February 1937 at the Benslow Nursing Home in Hitchin. Her father was a butcher in the Stevenage area at the time. She has a younger sister born in 1939 and a brother who was born in 1945.

Prudence attended Denbigh Road School and later the Luton Convent, and after leaving, trained in St. John's Wood in order to become a florist. It was whilst working at Headey Nurseries in Dunstable that she met and subsequently married her employer.

A voluntary worker for the National Trust for nine years, Prudence recently attended a garden party at Buckingham Palace to mark the centenary years of the formation of the Trust. Her Majesty the Queen and Prince Charles attended.

SARAH ANN HILLS (NÉE LOWE)

Sarah was born on 3 October 1900 in Cause End Road, Wootton, next door to the shop and the Star Public House. This property has since been demolished. Her grandmother's home was one of the four Yeoman's Cottages at Chennell's Farm, then owned by Mr Frossell, and it was from there that her mother moved to Cause End Road to live following her marriage. When Sarah was a year old her parents moved to Keeley, Wootton. Both parents were from Wootton, and father was a thatcher by trade. Sarah was only three years old when he died of pneumonia, leaving her mother to raise four children, Sarah being the youngest.

CLAUDE HORWOOD

Claude was born at 41 Biscot Road, Luton, on 7 August 1911. His grandfather was a chemist in Dunstable, and later worked at the Wootton and Webb pharmacy. He then had his own shop in Brunswick Street, Luton. Claude's father was apprenticed to Harts hat manufacturers and he eventually left Harts and started in business on his own as a travelling peddler of hats. As a hat salesman, he was unsuccessful. He travelled around by train, and Claude's mother told him that there was so little profit that once he had bought his three-monthly season ticket, there was very little left. Claude's mother was a machinist in the hat trade.

MARY JEFFS (NÉE COOLING)

Mary was born on 26 December 1893 in West Bromwich, Staffordshire, and came to Bedford in the 1920s to stay with an aunt who was living in Kempston. She only came for a holiday, but loved the place so much that she decided to stay. West Bromwich was the Black Country, all coal mines, and Bedford seemed a complete change, to her.

Mary's mother died at the age of twenty-five, when Mary was a young child, and she was raised by her father's mother in Warwickshire. She thinks her father worked in the iron foundries but is not sure. He was in the First World War and returned, but didn't live long afterwards. She was his only child.

Mary's grandfather was a farm worker. Her grandparents' home was in Butlers Marston, just a little hamlet about nine miles from Stratford-on-Avon.

This was hunting country, and the local hunt was the Warwickshire hounds. Lord Willoughby de Broke had a large country estate there: he did a lot of private work for the Queen Mother.

RICHARD THOMAS LOVELL

Richard, who was always known as Tom, was born at The Folleys in Clapham in August 1904, and was one of twelve children. Tom's family were keen sports people, but because of leg injuries systained in his younger days, Tom was never able to participate. One brother was a well-known professional boxer.

STANLEY GEORGE LOVELL

Stan was born on 9 March 1909 in Hall End, Wootton. He was one of three children, and his father was a general labourer – a bricklayer's labourer – who worked at the brickworks, and for Samuel Foster, the builders in Kempston, where Bushbys are now situated. He also worked for Mr Lunnis, the builder at 'Tags End' which is now called Cause End Road. After leaving school at fourteen, Stan worked at the local brickworks for many years.

Stan was in the St. John's Ambulance Brigade for twenty-five years, at Stewartby and then at Kempston, and only left the Brigade in 1954, when he was diagnosed as having a brain tumour. He received medical training in Sidmouth, Devon and was a male nurse with the RAF at Weeton near Blackpool and then at North Allerton, until he was demobbed. He helped to set it up, in North Allerton, and was there when the first patient arrived. It was like a general hospital for the Air Force. He chose this career course with the RAF because of his experience in the St. John's Ambulance Brigade.

ETHEL ANNIE MAYES (NÉE JARVIS)

Ethel was born in Luton on 30 August 1899. Her mother died when she was three, and, left with a family of six children, her father re-married. His second wife had been employed as a housekeeper in a big house. She looked after Annie and brought her up well: 'she was a very good person'. There were no children from this second marriage.

Ethel's husband had always worked for his uncle, who had a shop in Hastings Street (now the site of a block of offices) called Rumblows. They did watch and clock repairs. The uncle had no children and when he died he left the business to Ethel's husband. She and her two sons continued to run it for quite some time after the death of her husband. It was well-known locally.

WALTER REGINALD PARROTT

Walter, who has always been known as Reg, was born on 28 January 1901 in a stone and thatched cottage in the village of Milton Ernest.

Reg married in 1927 and set up home in Thurleigh. In 1959 he and his wife acquired a sixteen acre smallholding in Keysoe and planned to grow wheat crops and to use the straw for thatching. Despite the untimely death of his wife in 1963 at the age of 57, he carried on, but after retirement, returned to live in Milton Ernest in a little cottage overlooking the park where he had spent many happy hours in his younger days watching cricket. 'Living by myself was not my way of life, being one of a large family and a family man myself' (Reg was one of eleven children, and he and his wife had four children).

Subsequently Reg re-married, his new wife having been a neighbour and friend of long-standing. They lived in a stone and thatched cottage in Thurleigh Road, Milton Ernest, similar in many respects to the cottage in which Reg was born. From his cottage home he could see the church to the left, and on the right, on Church Green, the school, both of which he attended in his young days.

WILLIAM GEORGE FRANK PERRIDGE

Frank, as he has always been known, was born on 20 November 1901 in Southill, on Mr Samuel Whitbread's estate where the sawmills were run by his father, George, who originated in Silverstone, Northampton-shire. Frank left school when the war started, and after a couple of years on the farm, began work in the timber trade. During his time on the farm, there were only old men and boys available for work. He enjoyed working with horses, and helping with ploughing. For many years Frank worked with his father, who died in 1943. He has spent the remainder of his working life in the timber trade.

HILDA PHOEBE PUDDEPHATT

Hilda was born on 15 December 1891 in Luton, and grew up in Princess Street. Her father was a straw hat manufacturer and owned his own small private factory which was built on one side of the garden. Both of her parents were Lutonians. They had one other child, a boy. Hilda's father died in 1915.

Hilda enjoyed her school days and attended Luton's first Grammar School on Park Square. She went on to teach, her first post being at Buxton Road Church School in 1909. She retired in 1957.

CONSTANCE RICHARDS (NÉE STANTON)

Connie was born on 8 July 1929 at Twinwoods, where her farm-worker father occupied a cottage belonging to Sidney Quimby, who owned Brownswood Farms. She had one brother who died soon after birth. The family moved to Milton Ernest when she was three-and-a-half, as the farmer wanted the house which her parents lived in. She remained in Milton Ernest until she married, and now lives in Oakley.

Connie's enduring hobby is her involvement with the Eighth Air Force historical Society. She has amassed a great deal of information, pictorial and otherwise, and memorabilia associated with the war period and the Americans serving in this country. She is an authority on such matters and is dedicated to the task of perpetuating memories of a time she knew as an innocent and impressionable young village girl.

CONSTANCE MARIE ROBINSON (NÉE SAUNDERS)

Connie was born at 21 Bedford Road, Wootton, on Christmas Day in 1909, which is why she was given the name 'Marie'. She was one of eight children, and her parents had a smallholding at their Bedford Road home.

Connie became a teacher, and her first permanent teaching post was at Wootton Primary School, where she herself had once been a pupil.

PERCIVAL GEOFFREY SHERWOOD

'Geoff' was born at 17 Battison Street, Bedford on 27 May 1919. Owing to the fact that his father's brother was also called Percival, he was always known as Geoff, and still is. His father was an electrical engineer, and his father before him was a blacksmith engineer on the Railway. After leaving Queen's Park School in 1934, he was employed at the Igranic Company in Bedford from 1934 to 1942, when he was conscripted, but returned to his employer and was then engaged on priority work for the war effort. After other assignments, he returned to the Igranic in 1946. He was Chief Fire Officer of the Igranic Fire Brigade from 1950 until 1968, when it was disbanded, a member of the Works First Aid Party, and also a member of the Civil Defence Rescue Team and held a 'Gold Star' Civil Defence Rescue Instructor's Certificate. He was also a member of the Bedfordshire Ambulance Team. It was not until 1970 that he took responsibility for his father's antiques business, but he has always been connected with it. His hobbies over the years have included bowls, darts, skittles, fishing and gardening.

EVELINE STANTON

Eveline was born on 10 February 1897 in Colmworth village. There were eight children in the family, five boys and three girls. She had more illness than any of the other children, yet outlived them all.

After a prolonged illness whilst in her teens, Eveline took up poultry farming – her doctor's suggestion. She would have preferred nursing, but felt she hadn't sufficient strength to cope with the demands of nursing.

ARTHUR 'LOL' LAWRENCE THEW

'Lol', as he was always known, was born on 31 October 1903 in the end one of three cottages in Harrold High Street, which stood opposite the present garage. There were three children in the family, and his father worked in the leather trade. His grandfather was a shepherd.

After leaving school at 13, Lol wanted to join the airforce, which he could not do until the age of fifteen. He did get as far as London in an attempt to join up, but failed because of his poor eyesight. He also wanted to go to Australia, but could not because his mother would not consent. He subsequently joined his father in the leather industry.

ERIC THORNE

Eric was born on 9 January 1896 in Woburn and was the third child of five. His father owned a butcher's shop in High Street North, Dunstable, at one time, and was always connected with farming and animals.

In 1921 Eric and his brother Cyril sailed to Australia. It was a very hard life and they had to do odd jobs to earn a living. They slept rough many times, not having sufficient money to pay for lodgings. At one time Eric rode a horse in a race and also entered the boxing ring as a contestant, to make money. Cyril met a girl and settled down, but although Eric was not afraid of hard work, he gave up and came home after two years. A year later he married Maude Durante of Houghton Road and settled down in Markyate where their son Frank was born. In 1930 he bought a piece of land in Beale Street from his father and had a house built, in which he lived until his death in 1985.

JOHN 'JACK' CLIFFORD THORNE

Jack, as he has always been known, was born on 2 April 1907 in Ilford, Essex. His father, a monumental mason, was killed in a road accident involving horses, whilst cycling to work. The fourth child in the family was born shortly after the death of his father, and Jack's mother then returned to live near her parents at Cross End, Thurleigh.

Jack, who regards himself as being self-educated, started work on the farm, and went on to do nursery gardening, and then became a gardening chauffeur, which he describes as the best job he ever had. His employers were wealthy people but very nice people who treated him as a 'human being'. He farmed out of necessity, but points out that farming at that time was poorly paid, and carried low status.

GLADYS LILLIAN WALLIS (NÉE FROST)

Gladys was born on 28 August 1904 in Bassingbourne, Cambridgeshire, which is near Royston. There were seven children in the family, of whom six survived, and her father was a police constable. Gladys's maternal grandfather was a blacksmith by trade, but her grandparents also had a small market garden. They lived in Soham in the Fens, between Ely and Cambridge.

Gladys's parents moved around as her

father was posted in different places, but she started school in Bassingbourne and 'loved every minute of it'. She went on to become a teacher herself. She married at twenty-five, and met her husband in the village where she first went to teach. He had just come out of the army when she first knew him and after their marriage, they set up home in Maulden, where she has lived since 1929.

BEATRICE MAY WEBB (NÉE JEFFORD)

 May, as she has always been known, was born in Hounslow, Middlesex, on 28 July 1906. Her father was Haynes born, and this is where all of his family lived. At the time May was born, he was working as a builder's labourer – a yard-man – in Chiswick, and when he was drafted into the army in 1914, her mother moved back to Haynes to be near his family. May's mother was born in Wiltshire, but had been in service in Hounslow before their marriage.

May's father was killed in action on 4 November 1918, a few days before the armistice was signed.

May's husband's family came from near Biggleswade, where his father was a smallholder. He and his parents moved to May's present cottage home in 1919, and they married in 1933. Her mother-in-law was an independent lady who worked on the land and continued to do so until she was in her seventies, at which time she qualified for a pension. May's husband was a farm worker all his life.

HORACE GEORGE WELCH

Horace was born in Stagsden West End on 25 October 1907, in his father's small tied cottage. His father was a horse keeper to a local farmer. There were eleven children in the family, eight of whom were born in this cottage. Horace eventually took over his father's cottage, and four of his own children were born there. His mother died aged eighty-seven, and his father at eighty.

When Horace retired from farming, he applied for a Council house and was eventually housed at Wood End, Kempston.

OLIVER WELLS

Oliver, the youngest of nine children, was born at Felmersham Grange, Felmersham, on 10 March 1922. The Wells family are well-known for their business interests, being based in Bedford. Oliver maintains that there was never any pressure on him to join the family business – Charles Wells Ltd. – founded by his grandfather in 1876. Ever since his inaugural flight in a DH Moth at the age of ten, his main ambition was to fly. Having left Uppingham at the age of eighteen, he joined the Royal Air Force and gained great satisfaction from being able to fly. Oliver left the Forces in 1956, shortly before the death of his father. Following his father's death he was obliged to help in the business.

Wing Commander Wells was awarded an OBE in 1992 for services to the community in Bedfordshire.

FREDERICK WALLACE WILDMAN

Fred was born on 27 August 1893 at 1 Cross End, Thurleigh. He was the eldest of seven children and was born in the house in which his grandmother was born and where his parents set up home when they married. Fred's father was a carpenter, wheelwright and undertaker. Fred worked for his father before leaving school, and after leaving school at twelve. In later life he was a very energetic member of his community – in particular within the Church, the Cricket Club, in fund-raising and so on.

Fred lived an active and long life, and enjoyed good health. At the age of ninety-four he was breaking bricks to lay a new driveway!

ALEC WILFRID WILMOT

Alec was born on 29 March 1913 in Southill and has worked all his life as a piano tuner/repairer. He married in 1939 and had one daughter Sandra, who has been very supportive.

He and his wife Gwen have shared many interests including cycling, dancing, walking, and camping. He regularly attends Yoga, enjoys 'keep fit', aerobics and swimming. Since losing his wife three years ago, he has been an active supporter of various charitable causes, and has established the Gwen Wilmot Alzheimer's Memorial Fund, to which he contributes money each year on the anniversary of her death from Alzheimer's Disease.

THOMAS WILLIAM WOODCOCK

Tom was born on 27 December 1910 in a cottage in Old Bedford Road, Luton, his maternal grandmother's home. He was raised by his grandmother, who 'adopted' him 'on the spot'. His grandfather was an Irishman, who was lost at sea, and his grandmother remarried a Mr Stevens. At school Tom was known as Tommy Stevens. His mother worked in munitions during the First War, and remarried after the war. His grandfather died when he was ten, and Tom was very upset, and knew he'd lost a 'good old pal'. His grandfather took care of him, took him fishing and bird catching along the back garden. His grandmother cooked sparrow pie, about a dozen birds to one pie. Tom recalls that there was always a fight when his grandad killed something to eat – duck, rabbit, chicken – and he refused to eat anything his grandfather killed.

Tom married in June 1939 and set up home in Wheathampstead in Hertfordshire, from where he cycled to work in Chaul End Lane, Luton, every day. He spent most of his working life in the foundries of Luton, where he worked as an iron moulder.

Index to Locations

Books Published by
THE BOOK CASTLE

JOURNEYS INTO BEDFORDSHIRE: Anthony Mackay.
Foreword by The Marquess of Tavistock, Woburn Abbey.
A lavish book of over 150 evocative ink drawings.

LEGACIES:
Tales and Legends of Bedfordshire and Hertfordshire:
Vic Lea. Twenty-five mysteries and stories based on fact, including
Luton Town Football Club. Many photographs.

MANORS and MAYHEM, PAUPERS and POLITICS:
Tales from Four Shires: Beds., Bucks., Herts., and Northants.:
John Houghton.
Little-known historical snippets and stories.

BOURNE and BRED:
A Dunstable Boyhood Between the Wars: Colin Bourne.
An elegantly written, well-illustrated book capturing the spirit of
the town over fifty years ago.

BEDFORDSHIRE'S YESTERYEARS Vol. 1:
The Family, Childhood and Schooldays: Brenda Fraser-Newstead.
Unusual early 20th century reminiscences, with private photographs.

BEDFORDSHIRE'S YESTERYEARS Vol. 2:
The Rural Scene: Brenda Fraser-Newstead.
Vivid first-hand accounts of country life two or three generations ago.

BEDFORDSHIRE'S YESTERYEARS Vol. 3:
Craftsmen and Trades People: Brenda Fraser-Newstead.
Fascinating recollections over several generations practising many
vanishing crafts and trades.

BEDFORDSHIRE'S YESTERYEARS Vol. 4:
War Times and Civil Matters: Brenda Faser-Newstead.
Two World Wars, plus transport, law and order, etc.

BETWEEN THE HILLS:
The Story of Lilley, a Chiltern Village: Roy Pinnock.
A priceless piece of our heritage – the rural beauty remains but the
customs and way of life described here have largely disappeared.

GLEANINGS REVISITED: Nostalgic Thoughts of
a Bedfordshire's Farmer's Boy: E. W. O'Dell.
His own sketches and early photographs adorn this lively account
of rural Bedfordshire in days gone by.

FARM OF MY CHILDHOOD, 1925–1947: Mary Roberts.
An almost vanished lifestyle on a remote farm near Flitwick.

Further titles are in preparation.
All the above are available via any bookshop, or from the
publisher and bookseller

THE BOOK CASTLE
12 Church Street, Dunstable Bedfordshire, LU5 4RU
Tel: (01582) 605670